to Be my brot recovry. Rev. Pierre

Immanuel
(God with us)
in Recovery

Hope and direction for people in recovery

By Pierre Leroux

Shoemaker, S., Minirth, Dr. F., Fowler, Dr. R., Newman, Dr. B. and Carter D. *Steps to a New Beginning*. Nashville: Thomas Nelson Inc., 1992.

www.BibleGateway.com

www.biblestudytools.com

Although the author has made every effort to ensure the accuracy and completeness of information contained in this book, he assumes no responsibility for errors, inaccuracies, omissions, or any inconsistency herein. All scripture has been lifted completely intact from its source. Any slighting of people, places, or organizations is unintentional.

www.xulonpress.com

Table of Contents

Introduction vii

Acknowledgments xiii

Chapter 1 – From Mess to Messenger 15

Chapter 2 – Preaching Recovery 35

Chapter 3 – Following Jesus 55

Chapter 4 – The Good is Often the Enemy of the Best 76

Chapter 5 – The Starting Point 85

Chapter 6 – Denial and Addiction 96

The 12 Steps and How They Work 106

Chapter 7 – We Admit That We Need Help! 110

Chapter 8 – We Begin to Hope 129

Chapter 9 – We Choose Life 140

Chapter 10 – We Investigate 145

Chapter 11 – We Confess 153

Chapter 12 – We Repent 157

Chapter 13 – We Humble Ourselves............................ 162

Chapter 14 – We Become Accountable 168

Chapter 15 – We Rebuild Relationships 174

Chapter 16 – We Practise Accountability 180

Chapter 17 – We Seek After Him................................ 185

Chapter 18 – We Carry the Message.......................... 194

Chapter 19 – Preventing Relapse 203

Chapter 20 – A New Beginning................................... 210

Introduction

When I decided to quit using alcohol and drugs and "stay quit," I had no idea the path I was heading down would lead to the healing of my mind, soul and spirit. Early in recovery, I was filled with the desire to help others find freedom from their addictions. I wanted other addicts to realize their insane lifestyle could be traded for a hopeful future.

As I went to meetings, got a sponsor and worked the 12 Steps of Alcoholics Anonymous and Narcotics Anonymous, I stayed clean and sober and decided to turn my will and life over to the care of God the Father through His Son, Jesus Christ. Later, by working the steps, I became accountable and accepted responsibility for my past and present behaviours. I made amends to the people I hurt, and with personal choices and God's power, I was able to forgive my enemies.

By working the 12 Steps, I was guided into an intimacy with God through His Son, Jesus Christ. By living the steps, I worked at passing on what I had learned – to comfort others with the same comfort I received from God.

After quite a few years of successful recovery, in my longing to grow as a Christian, I came back to the Church. Even though the Church had been an unsafe place for me in the past, my yearning to draw closer to my higher power, the God of my understanding, was stronger than my fears. As I matured with one foot in the recovery community and one in the Church community, I noticed resistance from both communities to embrace each other, even though they have their origins through the intervention of Jesus Christ.

A big part of the recovery community at meetings discourages personal sharing on the benefits of following Jesus, or as one of the founders of AA, Bill Wilson, calls his "higher power," "the God of the preachers." This limits growth and creates frustration and confusion for Christians in recovery who are experiencing the benefits of the 12 Steps.

The Church communities (usually the ones who are the loudest) are suspicious and resistant to the 12-Step recovery community way of doing things, especially the lack of specifics when it comes to the words "higher power" and "the God of Your Understanding." Some of them even go so far as to resent the fact there is a recovery community. I have come to understand that those who resist or resent the success of those fellowships are either angry that those people aren't coming to church to find freedom, or are angry with past or present addicted family member(s) who have or are still causing them frustration and grief.

Even though people in recovery have repented from their addiction, some in the Church view them through the eyes of the older brother in the story of the Prodigal Son. This lack of mercy and compassion creates a lack of acceptance and an atmosphere of condemnation for the Christian who struggles in recovery. They will sometimes choose to leave the Church and return to the safety and acceptance of the 12-Step fellowships.

What follows is an attempt to help bridge the Church and Christians who are part of the 12-Step culture. My personal testimony of God's mercy and healing grace coupled with 12-Step exercises was written for both new and mature Christians in recovery. It's written for Church leadership staff and volunteers who will learn of the beginnings of the AA fellowship and the integrity of the steps as they relate to the scriptures. It's also written for Christian family members and friends of the addict to encourage a better understanding surrounding the problems and perseverance needed to stay clean and sober.

As you read, investigate and hopefully apply some of this information, allow me to encourage you not to focus on the things you disagree with or don't understand. For your own benefit, push through. Take what you can and leave the rest.

As someone who has worked the steps and experienced their benefits I would like to encourage you to persevere and follow through. The results will be a sense of freedom like you have never experienced before.

May God the Father and His Son, Jesus Christ, bless you and your family as you seek to free yourself and help others find freedom from the bondage of addiction.

Rev. Pierre Leroux CACII

Acknowledgments

I want to thank my wife, Joyce, and my sons Joseph, Isaiah and Isaac for their prayers and encouragement. I thank them for their patience, especially during those times when I experienced doubt, frustration and confusion.

I'm grateful to the fellowships of Alcoholics Anonymous and Narcotics Anonymous where I have found an abundance of knowledge and support for the last 28 years. I want to acknowledge all the various Christians and non-Christian recovery facilities I've had the privilege to work and minister at. I want to thank the leadership, staff, residents, clients and patients of those facilities for the challenges, the knowledge and wisdom I was able to glean from those relationships – all of which have helped me in writing this book.

After more than 25 years of walking with Christ and ministering in the recovery fields, I've learned through many venues – seminars, DVDs, CDs and cassette teachings, radio and TV programs, sermons, Bible school, Bible colleges, etc. The writing that follows is a blending of personal ideas, experience and learned material. So to all of you, thank you!

Finally, it needs to be said this would not have been possible without the guidance and wisdom of Immanuel (God with us) In Recovery.

Chapter 1

From Mess to Messenger

If God loves me so much, why did I not start experiencing His love until much later in life?

I was born in Montréal and grew up in a middle-class family. My father worked hard and loved his wife and children. I was the middle child, sandwiched between my older sister and younger brother.

Have you ever had a relationship with someone that is not quite what you would like it to be? That's what my relationship with my mother was like. At a young age, I could sense she had a difficult time being around me. The acceptance she had with my sister and brother was very different from the one I experienced with her. I could sense her resentment from an early age. For a while, I tried to please her in various ways, hoping to get more affection from her. I'm not sure how old I was when I started fearing she was going to abandon me. I remember coming home after school one day and I was alone in the house. I was sure she and the rest of the family had left me. Of course, it wasn't true. A little later, my mother and sister showed up. They had gone to the grocery store. I remember their laughter at my tears when I told them I thought they had gone for good.

With my father, it was different. I could tell from his behaviour towards me that he cared. Even though at the ages of five or six we were discouraged to kiss or hug him, there were other times in my youth when he would slip me a few dollars as a demonstration of his love – or at least that's the way I took it.

As for my brother, the envy I felt towards him because of the attention and love he received from my mother made him my adversary, so I avoided him. My sister did care for me, but it's fair to say I didn't know how to love her back. By the time I was a teenager, my ability to experience or accept love was almost non-existent. I grew

in a self-centred self-pity, and my world got smaller and smaller.

A few years back, my brother sent me a family picture from

the time before I was seven years old. You can see in the picture

a happy boy making faces who seems to be experiencing life to its

fullest. I found it interesting, looking at the picture, that I couldn't

recognize – or remember – the clowned-face child.

One of the biggest challenges for my whole family was the pro-

gression of Dad's addiction to alcohol. He became a binge drinker

and it almost destroyed our whole family. My father had been on

his own since he was 13 and had worked hard most of his life. He

was a thinker, an introvert mostly, who seemed to come out after

a few drinks. I remember my mom and dad dancing together at a

family gathering and having what seemed to be a lot of fun. Then

later on that evening, I recall my father in drunken stupor smashing

furniture. As his drinking progressed, there were more violent epi-

sodes, but mostly at home. Those incidents really messed me up mentally and emotionally, and I became fearful of being around him, especially when he was drinking.

When he came home after a drinking bout, my mother's way of trying to cope was to attack him verbally. My father's way of trying to shut her up was to smash things, which eventually progressed to attacking her physically, and anyone else who came between him and his target. It was a terrible time. There were malicious screaming matches which kept us children awake most of the night. I wondered at times how two people who said they loved each other could treat each other that way. Being the more sensitive and dramatic child of the three, when my father went out at night, I would be unable to sleep until he was back in the house and asleep, even if his outing was legitimate.

Sometimes, after a violent episode, my mother would pack us up and take us to a shelter for the night. Other times, my mother would only take my sister and brother with her, and left me with my dad. Those times were terrifying for me. Even though this created a bond between my dad and I, I hated being left behind. This only increased my sense of feeling unloved and unimportant.

I don't blame my parents. I don't believe my father chose to become a violent alcoholic, and I know my mother didn't realize she resented me. I believe both my parents did the best they could with the tools they had. However, that atmosphere created havoc with my mind and emotions.

As a French Canadian living in Québec in the late '50s, religion was part of life. I went to Catholic school, was part of the choir and served Mass. We prayed together on weeknights as a family from 7:00 to 7:15, reciting the rosary with Cardinal Léger on the radio. During some of my times of turmoil, I would go to the church building where at times I would find peace. I would ask God in fear to tell me what kind of plan He had for my life. I didn't know Him as a loving God. Later on in my adult life, I wondered why I never heard about Jesus' saving love or forgiveness. The emphasis on praying to the Virgin Mary was so strong in those days, I missed the real Good News of God. Scripture says, "For by the power of the eternal Spirit,

Christ offered himself to God as a perfect sacrifice for our sins. That is why he is the one who mediates a new covenant between God and people, so that all who are called can receive the eternal inheritance God has promised them" (Hebrews 9:14-15, NLT). I was led to believe Mary was the mediator between us and God. So as a child, I would pray to her. I remember being told by someone from the clergy if I recited three "Hail Mary's" and one "Act of Contrition" every night, at my time of death the Holy Virgin would send a priest to my side so I could be freed of all my sins.

Being part of a Cub Scout troop for two years kept me from completely losing my mind. The female leaders were not only encouraging and affectionate, but one of them was also the most beautiful young lady I had ever seen as I was entering puberty. After Cubs, I joined the Boy Scouts of Canada, where I continued to feel accepted and supported. My physical abilities in sports made me stand out, and helped with my poor self-esteem.

Later on, during an interview with the chaplain of our troop, a "Black Robe," I realized by his physical touch that the interview was only a pretext for his pedophile assault on little boys. I tried to tell my leaders what this man had tried to do, but no one believed me or did anything about it. That summer at camp, when the chaplain showed up, my anger rose and I left the troop. Even though what happened to me at the hands of this clergyman was terrible, I believe that from a spiritual perspective, telling children to pray through the Virgin Mary instead of Jesus Christ is the worst sin of the two.

Those late pre-teen and early teen years were very confusing, both emotionally and sexually. Prior to the sexual assault by the chaplain, I had been raped by a judo instructor. What made it worse was that I got set up by one of my best friends, who announced to me he was a homosexual. I was naïve in those days compared to most people. My friend, who had just stolen a car, suggested we go to the judo instructor's home. There, he said, we would probably find beer to drink. After we got there, my friend excused himself, saying he had to go to the store. While he was gone, I was raped.

When my friend came back to the apartment, in my embarrassment, I said nothing. Only later did I realize I had been set up.

When I was thirteen, a single mom in her late teens invited me to her home with the pretext of drinking together. After a while she offered herself to me, trying to teach me the basics of sex. She was the picture of crudeness, which skewed my understanding of what women and lovemaking was really like.

By now I was lying to my parents about a lot of things, including going to church on Sunday. Usually I spent church time across the street at a restaurant. Drinking had become more important and since I was working part-time with my father, I had money to drink. I also became a petty thief, which helped supply funds to buy more booze. I even went so far as to sell myself to another man to buy beer, which was a terrible experience thanks to my past trauma with people of the same sex.

Some of the boys I hung around with were members of a little gang in Montréal. Even though I did some crimes with them, I wasn't good gang material. I was too sensitive and naïve. I liked hanging with them – some of the things we did were scary and exciting. When I was 16, two of the gang members who were going out with twin sisters invited the rest of us to have our way with the girls – basically, to rape them. I refused to participate and tried to influence the others to do the same, but to no avail. I never associated with those guys again.

So my teen years were filled with turmoil at home, school problems, drinking, girls and confusion. I left school in Grade 11 and went to work as a helper on a truck for an electrical company. My next job was unloading 50- and 100-pound sugar bags from freight cars. At 19, I applied and was accepted in the Canadian Armed Forces. To say the least, my drinking, partying and promiscuity reached a new level of intensity. I was a transport operator who moonlighted as a bouncer at the Airmen's Club.

At the club, I fought pretty well every night, never losing a fight for more than 18 months. It's not that I was a good fighter. All the unexpressed rage inside me came out through my fists, which knocked out my opponents most of the time. I often felt remorse after drinking and fighting, and would sometimes even apologize to those I had beaten up the night before.

In my early 20s, after drinking three bottles of red wine, I blacked out (chemically induced amnesia). During the blackout, I gravely insulted my girlfriend of two years and demolished the motel we were staying in. The next morning, we were asked to leave. So we all got in our cars and decided to go to the beach to continue partying. When we got there, I jumped out of my friend's convertible, ran to the beach, and into water. Showing off, I tried to arc my body backwards and then spring forwards to make a big splash as I dove in. Suddenly, I felt a dull pain at the top of my head, lost consciousness and began to drown. My friends pulled me out of the water and carried me to the beach where I came to. The burning pain through my body was excruciating, and I was unable to move from the neck down.

After two hospitals and a multitude of x-rays, I was diagnosed with two crushed vertebrae in my neck. The first 17 days were a blur. Every three to four hours, I was given pain medication intravenously to help me deal with the trauma. I do remember waking up in-between injections and seeing my family who had driven more than 300 kilometres to visit me. I was so drugged up, I fell back to sleep. In my impaired state I couldn't understand why they would go out of their way and drive so far just to see me. It's interesting that I never called out to God during those difficult times. I did call out to the nurses each time they were late with my injection.

After the first operation, I was able to move again, but in my medicated state, when I got out of bed all excited, I slipped and fell against the bed. I destroyed all the work the doctors had tried to do with the first surgery. So after an attempt at traction which failed, it was decided that another surgery was needed. This time, the doctor fused and wired bone grafts in my neck.

It's obvious to me now this is where my addiction began. During my stay in hospital, I lost 40 pounds. So it was decided I should be given a few beers before every meal to help me gain weight. So I had beer, drugs and good-looking nurses, which wasn't bad for a while.

I didn't realize at the time how important drugs had become to me. I was full of anticipation before getting my medication. I looked forward to the contentment I would experience when the medication would kick in. It had become my higher power – and I didn't even know it.

On the bright side, I was encouraged when the people I used to hang around with at the Air Force base came to visit. They had taken up a collection at the Airmen's Club and bought all kinds of gifts for me. Some of the girls had baked a cake with green icing in the shape of a frog. (In those days, my nickname was "Pete the Frog.")

The gratitude and emotions I felt at the time is hard to describe. I do recall feeling overwhelmed and crying. It was confusing for me, since the only time I felt worthy of receiving affection or love was when I had done something to deserve it – in other words, worked for it. Here, I felt helpless. I was weak. I couldn't perform and was the recipient of all these gifts and affection, all this grace.

The analogy of God's love for us is obvious today. God doesn't love us because we deserve it, or because we worked for it. He brings us the gifts of mercy and grace in the forgiveness of sins, through His Son. Jesus was punished, beaten for our sins so that we would experience peace. Like any gift, the only thing we can do when it's presented to us, is to believe that it **is** for us, and receive it.

After being released from the hospital, I was on a lot of muscle relaxants and painkillers, some of which mixed well with alcohol. As my addiction progressed, so did my tolerance for mood-altering chemicals. I started experimenting with street drugs to increase the painkilling effects, but it only lasted for a short while. With the frustration of constant pain, I became more violent and destructive. After a few incidents, I was asked to leave the Armed Forces with an honourable discharge. I wasn't given a choice – I was told either to take my release or be asked to leave. I was devastated at first. In my self-centredness, I couldn't understand why so drastic a measure was taken. So I left Ontario. I drove a Bluebird school bus from the factory to Alberta, then took a Greyhound bus and ended up in Duncan on Vancouver Island, British Columbia.

As a young boy in Montréal, I had experience working with lumber when I worked with my father, so I found work in a sawmill working on a green chain separating and piling lumber. It was good physical hard work and I enjoyed it. The money was good and after a year at the mill, I was driving forklifts and lumber carriers.

My first marriage was to an air woman I had been going out with while I was in Ontario. She had completed her service and followed me out West. She was also messed up from her past, but healthier than I was. She was trying to change her life – I wasn't. She often got jealous. She had seen me perform back at CFB Trenton, and assumed there were other women in my life. There were, but only as friends. Her jealousy was overwhelming at times.

By now, I was drinking more often, taking pills, and getting more and more depressed. I was on antidepressants and started to have mild anxiety attacks. I was hallucinating, and the pictures I saw were demonic. In one of my psychotic episodes, I tried to kill my wife. When she screamed, I came out of my state and realized there was something wrong with me. So I signed myself into a psychiatric ward. My wife did try to help me for a while, but it was too difficult for her. I was in and out of hospitals. I was drinking, having anxiety attacks, tried to commit suicide. I was a mess. I got home one morning after partying all night, and found out my wife had left me. I never saw her again. Later on, I found out she had found someone else.

The next few years saw more suicide attempts, psychiatric wards, anxiety attacks, lost jobs and financial problems. I was trying to deal with a broken heart through drugs and alcohol.

After a period of time, I decided to leave British Columbia and go back to Montréal, thinking if I changed towns, things would get better. I got a job working as a bouncer in one of the biggest clubs in downtown Montréal. On weekends, we packed in 700-800 people a night. I didn't know when I applied it was a gay bar. Not everyone who went there was gay. I would say most of the staff were straight. After the interviewer made me aware of the situation, I told him it wouldn't be a problem. I was wrong! I was around so much sexual perversion, and was given so much free booze and drugs, I got "twisted." It was a place with a lot of predators, and I acted nice to them, to get tips, free drugs or booze. Some of the friends I made there were good people. But let's face it: The main reasons people go to those places are to get loaded and score. As women offered themselves to me, I became more promiscuous. As the head bouncer during the week, I was showered with all kinds of drugs and free cognacs, but it became too much. I was getting drunk and stoned every night. On Halloween night, I quit.

Later that month, I drove back to Vancouver Island and started working in sawmills again. By then I was doing cocaine and alcohol. I loved MDA, but my favourite drug was Dexedrine. On "Dexies," I felt in control and content. I would go for days without sleep. I loved everyone I met, and felt at peace most of the time. But the withdrawals were terrible with severe depression and overwhelming feelings of despair with suicidal tendencies.

Then a sign of daylight! After many failed relationships, I met and moved in with a woman who had two children, a boy and a girl. After the normal resistance from the children, I was able to develop a relationship with them. Their mother was an intelligent, beautiful woman who had her issues, but again, compared to me, had her life together. She had succeeded in raising her children properly. She had her own house, and wasn't a full-fledged alcoholic or addict. We drank together, and I even got her to try cocaine once, but she didn't like it. After a while, she wanted me to quit doing drugs. I wanted her to stop telling me to quit. We'd argue about the children, about money. We were two strong, controlling people, and when we drank together, we'd argue intensely. For the first time, I was experiencing family life, although in retrospect that relationship was similar to the relationship that my mother had with my father.

One night, late in the evening while we were drinking and arguing, the young girl came down the stairs, crying. She thought we were arguing about her. We weren't. We just argued when we drank.

The state that young girl was in hit me hard. For the first time, I saw how my drinking and drugging were affecting the people I cared for. I had recreated the environment I was raised in. I had hit rock bottom.

In the next few days, I made an appointment to see an alcohol and drug counsellor in Duncan. After the normal resistance, I chose to enter a 28-day program in West Vancouver. On Saturday night, I drink a 26 ouncer of rye, and did about 20 codeine pills. The next evening, I entered treatment. I was a mess. I was coming down hard. My degree of anxiety was high. During treatment, I couldn't make out what the counsellors and educators were trying to teach us, and I really wanted to because I didn't want to fail. In-between sessions, I walked to try and regroup. I was terrified of group therapy, overwhelmed with the fear of being kicked out because of my lack of understanding. Half our group had quit or been asked to leave. It was a very anxious time. One night while in bed thinking, I had an anxiety attack. In desperation, I cried out to God, "If you're out there, I need help! Please help me!" The next morning, I felt different. I had more peace. I felt more confident, excited, and there was only one week left in treatment.

One of the staff at the centre was a night person who tried to make a point of talking with every client before they finished treatment. When he approached me and suggested we spend time together before I left, I was leery. We did end up together one evening, and he began to give me his spiel. I knew this was going to be about God. I don't remember what he said, but I do remember a part of me wanted to resist what God was doing through him by shutting down. I forced myself and let the message come in. I actually felt a part of me, that part that had been resisting God for all those years, leave me, as if it were an evil spirit.

I completed treatment and went back to my common-law relationship. I never drank again! I did relapse with medication – three times while trying to deal with physical pain, I went to the doctor who prescribed painkillers. I discovered my body doesn't differentiate between prescribed medication and street drugs. As soon as any kind of mood-altering chemical enters my system, the compulsion to take more than prescribed kicks in, and a few days later I've ingested the whole prescription. That's my definition of powerlessness.

After those relapses, I got involved with other people in recovery. I would go to the Alano Club, a restaurant meeting place for people in recovery. This is where I participated in my first meeting of Alcoholics Anonymous.

A few months later, I joined a Novalco group for recovering alcoholics. That was a close group, facilitated by a mature AA member, where the people involved would commit to working the 12 Steps of Alcoholics Anonymous using the Big Book and other AA literature for a period of four months. Although the literature talked only about alcohol addiction, I would mentally incorporate alcohol and drugs in the sentences where alcohol was mentioned.

In AA, in Step 3, it states: "We made a decision to turn our will and our lives over to the care of God *as we understood Him*." For me, like Bill Wilson, the founder of AA, that was the God of the preachers, The Father, through His Son, Jesus Christ. The Messenger!

Chapter 2

Preaching Recovery

After completing Novalco, I had some basic understanding and experience in living the steps. In Step 1, I admitted and practised the acceptance I could never use alcohol and drugs again. In Step 2, I had opened myself to the belief there is a God and He wants to help me. In Step 3, I surrendered my will and my life to the Father, Son and Holy Spirit. In Step 4, to the best of my abilities, I made a moral inventory of my life. In Step 5, I confessed to God and another person my moral inventory. In Step 6, I repented, turned to God and became willing to have Him change me. In Step 7, I asked God to forgive me and help me change because I couldn't do it by myself. In Step 8, I made a list of all the people I had harmed, and in Step 9 took steps to make things right. In practising Step 10 daily, I'm able to deal with the wreckage of the present. In Step 11 (my favourite), through prayer and meditation, I'm growing in the understanding of God's will and power, and direction for my life. And in Step 12, I had a strong passion to help others find freedom from their addiction.

I went to a lot of meetings. Even though AA is not a place to discuss other drug issues, I did use the meeting for that purpose. One day, while having coffee at the Alano Club with my sponsor, he shared with me that he knew of a fellowship in Victoria called Narcotics Anonymous which was specifically for drug addicts. The next day, I found out where the NA meetings were, and drove down to my first one. The atmosphere, openness and vulnerability gave me a sense of belonging I had never experienced anywhere. After a few months of driving to Victoria, I started two NA meetings in Duncan.

I rented an upstairs room at the Log Mart in Duncan. For the first time in a long time, I had purpose, I felt useful. I bought NA literature, promoted it, talked to alcohol and drug program coun-sellors, Social Services, and any other institution or free media I could find.

The meetings were every Friday and Saturday night. At first, of course, there was only me. I prayed to God He would bring people who needed help and, at the same time, I was afraid He would. During the week, I continued to drive to Victoria and participated in the NA meetings there.

Because of the accumulation of injuries I sustained while working in the lumber industry, I ended up on compensation and had a lot of time to help others. The Workmen's Compensation Board (WCB) was aware of my passion to help other addicts, and decided to help me by sponsoring some training to improve my skills. I took up Assessment and Interviewing, Primary Counselling Skills, Group Facilitating, and Alcohol and Drugs Overview. I felt blessed. I was receiving money from the WCB and helping others find freedom from their addictions. My injuries had become a gift.

So I continued to immerse myself in developing NA up-island. My goal was to have a meeting for every day of the week between Duncan and Nanaimo. It took about 18 months. On the home front, I married my common-law wife. We had a lot of problems. After three attempts at separation and reconciliation, I committed to staying away.

I found a place to live in Mill Bay. It was a beautiful cabin overlooking the ocean, and the road I lived on was called Whiskey Point. Go figure! The landlord and his wife were great people who had rebuilt and refurnished an old boathouse. I rented it for close to a year. I also bought my first new car. My little house on the ocean was a great place to experience God. It was a peaceful place filled with wildlife like birds, ducks, swans, seals and deer. At high tide, the water would slap the foundation of my cabin. The sound and rhythm of the waves were very therapeutic. I canoed a lot in those days. I would go for short trips around the bay, investigating God's beauty while giving Him thanks and praise for my life. The contrast of my red canoe with the black seals that followed me at times was amazing. During those canoe trips, most of my fears were pushed away by the excitement of experiencing God.

By 1995, the NA meetings in Duncan and Nanaimo were doing well. I tried to start some meetings in Mill Bay and Ladysmith, but they only lasted a short time due to lack of participation. However, the Nanaimo meetings were growing by leaps and bounds. There were three treatment centres in Nanaimo, and the involvement of their clients helped NA to grow there.

Needless to say, my love for the people in the fellowship was also growing. My desire to see them succeed and my strong personality would sometimes affect those relationships in a negative way. People who come to these meetings are often super-sensitive and very defiant, and my strong influence wasn't always received with openness. But what a crowd of special people they were. Most of them had gone through tragedies and survived. If you were to ask them in the beginning why they became addicts, the answers would vary. Some would say poor childhood, difficult upbringing, influences of others, abuse of some sort, but very few knew the real truth. It's interesting to hear how many would even blame God. In Proverbs 19:3 (NLT), it states: "People ruin their lives by their own foolishness and then are angry at the Lord." All of us got here because of rebellion, self-centredness, self-pity and resentment.

As I wrote this book, I couldn't help but recall some of the men and women I had the pleasure to meet in those early days of recovery. There were so many of them I loved and cared for, but I'm not sure I made it clear to them that I valued them a lot. There was so much self-centredness and anxiety in all our lives in those days. I don't believe any of us knew or could express genuine love to each other, but we did express acceptance and affection through our hugs.

Some of the bad choices and consequences of those early years had to do with allowing myself to be attracted to some of the women I was trying to help. My immaturity and naïveté was a perfect setup for the charm of a beautiful girl needing help with her recovery.

One of these women was a beautiful, enthusiastic lady 10 years my junior. At first, my intentions were good. She wanted help, and I wanted to help. But after a month, I started to experience a strong physical attraction to her looks and bubbly personality. About a month later, I told her I was having trouble staying detached. I must admit I was elated when she said she felt the same.

As soon as we opened that door, the power of lust and self-deception grew. I rationalized that because she was looking at Jesus for her higher power, that this relationship must've been from the Lord. It felt so right. It was a surreal time. I invited her to my place in Mill Bay and we started to spend a lot of time together. After a few overnight stays, my landlord suggested I start looking for a different place to live. He told me he wanted to remodel the cabin so his in-laws could use it during the summer. I did sense he was uncomfortable with my friend's overnight stays and so he found a pretext to ask me to leave. Eventually, my girlfriend and I found a place in Ladysmith. It was a logical choice, since it was between Duncan and

Nanaimo. From there, it was easier to oversee the growth of the NA fellowship.

After about three months of being together, I came home one evening and saw that my girlfriend was going through some emotional turmoil. I asked her what was wrong. She said, "You're going to hate me!" "Try me," I said. "I'm pregnant and I don't want the baby. I want an abortion!" I was shocked! I was confused. I believed I loved her and wanted to support her, but an abortion? That was wrong. This was my child growing in her. I didn't want it to be harmed. After a few days, she told me she wanted to go to Victoria to stay with her mother for a while so she could straighten things out in her mind. A week later, her mom called me and told me my girlfriend had had a miscarriage and had lost the child.

I drove to Victoria to see her. When she opened the door to her mother's apartment, she looked terribly depressed and extremely tired. She told me she wanted out of the relationship, and would come to Ladysmith and move her stuff out of the apartment. A week later, she did.

Losing both my girlfriend and my child was almost too much for me to bear. The temptation to go back using was so strong, but by the grace of God, I resisted.

"How did I get here?" I asked myself. "It felt so right. How could I have been so wrong?" I know today that when I close the door to God's ways, I opened the door to the evil one. Just because something *feels* right doesn't mean that it is. "For the Lord disciplines those he loves, and he punishes each one he accepts as his child" Hebrews 12:6 (NLT). The discipline (the teaching) was that He allowed me to follow my own path

I don't believe I really understood God's grace and mercy in those days. I knew I'd failed God, but I didn't know Jesus was beaten and punished so I could have peace. Intellectually, I believed that if I confessed my sins, I would be forgiven. My lack of understanding of the scriptures and the love of God lead me to believe I also had to perform to receive His forgiveness. In other words, I believed salvation was Jesus' death on a cross, and me doing something nice for God for others to be forgiven by Him. I didn't know any better. What a way to live!

After a period of grief and confusion, I refocused on God. I got a training position at a men's recovery centre in Courtenay, British Columbia. Part of my training included taking their six-week program, followed by an evaluation and supervised training. After only a few weeks, I was asked to take over a group session because one of the counsellors at the centre had resigned. The adjustment to my change of status for the clients was very difficult. Because of the poor timing and increased turmoil at the centre, it was suggested I move on and find another training position.

I found one with an employee assistance program in Duncan. It was great. I had a wonderful teacher who allowed me to suffer through my insecurities. A few months into the training, I became the EAP summer relief counsellor for Port Alberni, Campbell River, Vancouver and Duncan. The position lasted nine months. Then, I signed up for summer school at the Johnson Institute in Minneapolis, Minnesota. In the late '80s, the Johnson Institute was the place to go to get good training in the disciplines of intervention and addiction counselling. So for the next four months, I trained and upgraded my skills in the USA. My biggest realization at that summer school was I was already quite knowledgeable about addiction and the recovery process. Upon completion, I came back to Vancouver Island.

I decided to attend church with the hope of finding someone who was more mature in her walk with Jesus. Even though that was my initial motivator, I realized after a few weeks at church that God had used my desire for a new partner to get me involved with other Christians. Prior to this, I pictured myself differently from the people who attended church. Then, I met Joyce at a weekly Bible study. She was younger than me, attractive, and I was intrigued when I heard her talking to one of her friends about her beliefs regarding the importance of putting Christ first in all relationships, including marriage. Wow! That is what I had come to believe! After a few days, I got my courage up, prayed, and asked her to go out with me. She accepted. Three weeks later, I asked her to marry me.

She said she would postpone her answer until we got to know each other a bit more. We were from very different backgrounds. She was raised in the Christian Reformed Church. She was kind of quiet and knew very little about addiction. I found her non-judgemental attitude very attractive. She took people at face value. We fell in love and I must say it was very difficult to be away from her while I was training in various places.

I now needed to find work. In my lack of faith, I started screaming at God in frustration. It wasn't pretty, but at that exact moment, the phone rang. It was one of my recovery friends who knew I was looking for work. He told me about a new facility on the Sunshine Coast in British Columbia. They were looking for addiction counsellors. I went for an interview and got my first position as an addiction counsellor in a treatment facility.

So Joyce and I contacted our minister, got married, and moved to Sechelt. We rented a cabin overlooking the ocean. It was an old cabin, but we were on our honeymoon and the view was fantastic! Life with Joyce was good and exciting. She found a job as a travel agent, and I was part of the team developing a treatment program for the new facility. The owner/manager of the facility had a vision to fill the beds with high-profile people who struggled with addiction: lawyers, doctors, movie stars. Regarding wages, we were told we would start getting paid after we had clients residing at the centre.

The manager was a very flamboyant and controlling person. After a few months, we still had no clients. He started to overreact and fire staff. After a while, the only staff left was me. So we got pretty friendly, and he told me to hire other staff and promoted me to program co-ordinator. He gave me a month's salary, and we started to entertain referral agents. I tried my best to promote the centre, but anyone with any experience in the referral field would've been able to assess my lack of experience as a program co-ordinator. The manager became disappointed with me, and after a while I had a hard time reaching him or setting any kind of meeting with him.

Having been so excited at my new position in the beginning, I never took the time to look into the manager's credentials. I was so grateful for my first position as an addiction counsellor, I failed to notice my employer's grandiose and erratic behaviour. When he was overreacting and firing most of the staff, I should've picked up that there was more to this than meets the eye. When he promoted me to co-ordinator, I got to spend more time at the centre where his wife and son were also residing. I soon realized after listening to their frustrations that his behaviour showed symptoms of a late middle-stage alcoholic who was still drinking.

It was only after having trouble getting a meeting with him I realized to what degree my naïveté had influenced my judgement. I thought of doing an intervention, but to be successful I needed to find someone with the necessary influence and power to motivate the manager to quit. All I had was the wife and son who were afraid of his wrath, and a counsellor – me – who was owed by now more than $11,000 in back pay. I knew if I confronted him about his drinking, I would probably lose all that money. But I had to try!

He was receptive, and when I suggested he talk to his doctor about his symptoms, he was pleasantly agreeable. But he never did. After a few weeks, I resigned my position. I told him I couldn't continue to work at a recovery centre under the management of a practising alcoholic.

A few weeks passed and I got a call from the alcohol and drug program director in Nanaimo. He was looking for someone to start an NA meeting at the jail in Nanaimo. The position was for a part-time addiction counsellor. So we moved to Nanaimo. Again, Joyce got a job as a travel agent (I am so blessed to have her!). I started to work at Nanaimo Correctional Centre (NCC). Because of the departure of the alcohol and drug co-ordinator at the jail, I was promoted to that position after six months. Her departure almost destroyed our programs and relationships with the inmates. After a few months, I was able to rebuild some of those relationships and bring back credibility to our programs.

For more than six years, I co-ordinated the alcohol and drug programs at NCC. At first, I was very positive, hopeful and excited. But towards the end, I was becoming more and more cynical in dealing with that type of population. It was also during that time I became more disillusioned about the fellowship of NA. I had a stronger desire to see God glorified – and the opposite was happening.

The 12-Step fellowships are not a good place to grow in your understanding of the Father and His Son, Jesus Christ. Jesus says, "If any of you wants to be my follower, you must turn from your selfish ways, take up your cross, and follow me. If you try to hang on to your life, you will lose it. But if you give up your life for my sake, you will save it. And what do you benefit if you gain the whole world but lose your own soul? Is anything worth more than your soul?" (Matthew 16:24-26, NLT). What does it gain the recovering person to get sober and clean but lose his soul in the process? There is a difference between being spared and saved!

Being young in my faith and recovery, I thought getting clean and staying clean and sober was the message. So that's what I preached. I believe my intentions were good, but listen to what AA's Step 12 states: "Having had a spiritual awakening as a result of these Steps, we tried to carry this message to [other addicts], and to practise these principles in all our affairs." What is the message we carry? We've experienced a spiritual awakening. That by choosing to believe in God and opening ourselves to receiving from Him, we're set free. I only became aware of this fact later on in my recovery.

During those stressful times, I started going to Victoria when I needed renewal and relaxation. I would walk the seawall and talk to God. I loved feeling the wind and sea breeze against my face. It was like experiencing God's gentle power in a physical way. It filled me with joy. I would sometimes sit on the slopes overlooking the ocean and meditate. Other times, I would go to a Catholic church downtown and spend time praying.

It was during one of those trips I ran into Bob. I was going into the church and he was coming out. I had met Bob at the jail while he was incarcerated. We had developed a good friendship, and as his counsellor, I had referred him to a treatment centre because of his addictions. During our meetings at NCC, he being a Christian, we had read scriptures together, and shared our enthusiasm about walking with God. We had become very good friends.

In Victoria, he didn't even recognize me. He had relapsed and was demonstrating symptoms of "wet brain," a severe brain impairment caused by long-term alcohol abuse. Once you reach that stage, you can never be normal again.

He was drunk, dirty, and asking me for a cigarette. I bought him a pack at the corner store. I asked if he was hungry. He said he was. I took him to Denny's. He surveyed the pictures on the menu and asked if he could have a large bowl of pea soup. We ordered and when we got our food, he covered his soup with ketchup and started to eat. He smelled awful. Obviously, he was living on the streets and sleeping outdoors. I prayed to God that he would not notice the trouble I was having dealing with the odour. Here was somebody I really cared about and he didn't even recognize me. Then I saw earwigs come out of his jacket. The bugs had made a home in his coat. I started to sob. I had trouble holding back the tears. I don't think Bob even noticed.

Later, I took him to a shelter for the night. I asked if he wanted to pray together before he went in. He said no. I asked him if I could pray for him. With a spaced-out look in his eyes, he agreed. I think he was just being polite.

After I dropped him off, I reflected on what had just happened – especially the intensity of the sadness I experienced at the restaurant. I had been around hundreds of people in recovery, from all walks of life. Why so much sorrow this time?

The answer came to me. Jesus had granted me insight into His feeling regarding His lost sheep. He was allowing me to feel what He feels when someone He loves goes astray and is destroyed by reaping what they sowed. The sadness I felt for Bob was overwhelming. God has millions, maybe billions, of people who go astray. It must be terrible for Him.

About six months later, during another retreat to Victoria, I ran into an old-timer from NA. He was a Christian and had been very helpful to me in the beginning of my recovery. He said, "I hear your name mentioned up and down the island. You're evangelizing the island." I had never heard the word "evangelizing" used to describe my work with NA before. It kind of shocked me. Then, I reflected on what my evangelistic message had been: "Don't use, work the steps, get a sponsor, one day at a time, this too shall pass, whatever you do, don't pick up."

I don't think I ever mentioned to anyone I had had a spiritual awakening as a result of quitting. I never really understood the grace and forgiveness of God, so I never talked about it. I had just realized my evangelistic message was the wrong one. Jesus meets us in different places and settings, and as His followers, He tells us to go and make disciples of all nations (including the recovery nation), baptizing them in the name of the Father, the Son and the Holy Spirit, teaching them to obey all He has commanded. It was time to regroup.

Chapter 3

Following Jesus

In 1995, I successfully renegotiated my contract with the management at the jail in Nanaimo. It was only about a month later I experienced a strong pull to go to Bible school. Periodically, my wife and I had gone to Capernwray Harbour Bible School on Thetis Island for weekly retreats. During our time there, we found out they also provided a two-year theological program which included Christian leadership training. This exciting and scary desire was so illogical from the world's perspective, I thought it must have been from God. Later on that day, I discussed this with Joyce, who replied, "If God is calling you to go to Bible school, I guess we need to look into it." What a partner!

As for the logistics, wow! First, I needed to get out of the contract at the jail. Second, we needed to sell our home and make enough profit to support ourselves financially for two years. Third, we needed to find a place to live on Thetis Island. And fourth, we needed to put most of our furniture in storage. Oh, and we only had six weeks to do all this. To some, this would be overwhelming. But for Joyce and I, it was exciting because we knew through the peace we felt that God was in this – so it was up to Him to make it happen. We told some of our friends, but most of them were hesitant about our plans.

On Monday, I stuck my head inside the director's office at the jail to schedule a meeting for later on that day. When we met, I told him I wanted to resign. At first, he objected quite sternly, saying I didn't have that option. I continued to trust God, even though our meeting seemed to leave me no other option but to complete my contractual obligation. The next day in our lunchroom, I happened to be sitting beside the warden, my boss's boss. I asked him if we could get together after lunch to discuss something important to both of us. He was curious, and when I said I felt called by God to go to Bible school, he rationalized my change had more to do with mid-life crisis than a call from God. But he was gracious enough to let me go.

At my going-away party, I was given a great sendoff and a variety of gifts, one of which was a print of a painting called "The Angelus." No one could've known at the time that ever since I was a child, this had been my favourite painting. The picture shows a man and woman in the middle of their field, breaking from their work and taking time to pray at the sound of the noonday church bells. My dad actually paid a friend to paint a copy on canvas, which he hung in the hallway in our home in Montréal. I saw this coincidence (God incidence) as another confirmation we were doing the right thing in His eyes.

Then we had to sell our house in a poor market. For the first five weeks, no one even looked at the house. On the sixth week, it sold. Actually, the day we were moving and registering for the program on Thetis Island, the staff told us they had received a fax for us at the office. It was confirmation from our bank representative the money was in our account. Also, we were able to put most of our furniture in storage at my brother-in-law's place. Finally, we found a beautiful house right beside the ocean. I have a pastor friend who said recently he believes God likes the drama. I don't know why, but my experience is that He seems to.

September 1995 and the first day at Capernwray – what a contrast! Don't get me wrong. For the most part, I felt blessed to be working at the jail. I enjoyed my relationship with the staff and inmates, but it was a difficult environment to be in for a long period of time. I worked there for more than six years, and now I was shoulder to shoulder with mostly young people worshipping and learning about God.

We had a variety of teachers who came from India, the United States, England, Germany and Canada. I learned so much. We were asked to keep journals – two to four pages of personal observation on our weekly Bible lesson. Let me try to summarize what I learned that first year.

Righteousness in God's eyes is obtained by faith, not by works. Salvation is a gift from God – I can't earn it. I must choose to receive it and believe it. All the violence and wrath from God that I deserved because of my sinful nature and my sins were shouldered by the Lord Jesus on a cross more than 2000 years ago. I also came to believe and accept that a few days later, He was raised from the dead, and as a believer, I have received His Spirit that empowers me to live the Christian life when I depend on Him.

God has a plan. Regardless of what any of us are doing, He will bring it to completion, but He also invites us to get involved in building His Kingdom. The Bible teaches both the sovereignty of God and the responsibility of man. God is in control and man has choices – to put his trust in Jesus, and to forgive others. God will show mercy to those who ask for it. The longer we run away from Jesus, the longer we run away from the cure.

I need to practise unselfishness, to step away from myself, my plans, and pick up my cross daily and follow Him. The purpose of God for our lives is seldom clear. The unpredictability of following

Jesus is challenging. Count on it! Circumstances in my life do not *determine* who I am – they *reveal* who I am. In times of trouble, God will tolerate my honesty with Him. It's okay to complain to God about my circumstances, since His ways are so very different than mine, but I need to stay away from complaining about Him.

The Christian life is an adventure. Adventure means facing the unknown. We get to trust God, one day at a time, one situation at a time, knowing He is good and that He really values us.

As a follower of Jesus, I have different values, perspectives, ambitions and goals than the world or non-Christians. So yoking myself in marriage or business with non-believers will only cause trouble and confusion since my partner's values would be different than mine. My sense of identity and self-worth come from God. He has demonstrated by sending His Son to suffer and die for me that He values me a lot. I practised renewing my mind with God's estimates of me and others. Jesus has fulfilled all the laws of God for me and other believers, and because we received that grace and believe in it, we have peace with God. They didn't take Jesus' life. He gave it away.

We are all made in His image, creatures of God, but we're not all children of God. Only those who choose to receive and believe in the mercy and grace of God through His Son, Jesus Christ, become children of God. They are reborn. It is a godly fact that true repentance will be demonstrated in your life by a change of thinking that leads to a change of heart (affection). As I obey God in my Christian walk, my obedience will lead to His activity being demonstrated in my life.

My second year in Bible school was about Christian leadership. I learned the biggest servant in the family of God is the leader. I also learned the crowd does not bestow leadership on us – God does. Leaders need to practise loving others without expectations. We love others because Jesus loves them. The empowering gifts I get from God's Spirit are for others. When addressing sin in people's lives, the goal should be restoration, not condemnation. When listening to others, am I really listening, or just waiting to talk? The value of others is determined by the cost paid by God's Son for them.

Leaders need to know the objective of their ministry. When I complain about leaders who are over me, I'm actually saying to God, "I'm not sure I trust your decision of allowing him/her to be in charge."

Some of the scriptures that stood out the most during my two years at Capernwray Harbour were, "Choose for yourselves today whom you will serve … but as for me and my house, we will serve the Lord" (Joshua 24:15, NASB). God was encouraging me with the choice I was making.

" 'Not by might nor by power, but by My Spirit,' says the Lord of hosts" (Zachariah 4:6, NASB). He is saying He'll bring His plan to completion. My role is to trust Him. The battle belongs to the Lord; my part is to be available and obedient. "Only in returning to me and resting in me will you be saved. In quietness and confidence is your strength" (Isaiah 30:15, NLT).

We're saved by faith, we continue by faith. God is on my side. He's my helper. He's the Saviour of every situation in my life.

God used my troubles in life to show himself more real to me. One example that stands out happened during the second year of my training. There were 16 of us being trained for Christian leadership. A few weeks into our training, we were told we were going on a trip. We were not told where or for how long. When the time came to leave, we got into two vans, took ferries to Vancouver, and drove north into British Columbia. For three nights, we lived in a mountain cave. On the fourth day, we were taken to a big rock about five metres high and told to climb. Unbeknownst to my leaders, one of my biggest fears was heights. As a child, while attempting to climb a mountain near my home, I froze and it took a long time for me to move again and climb down. So when my leaders asked me to climb this big rock, I was obedient even though I was very fearful. After everyone had a turn, we were taken to a cliff where we could see someone had already set up rope for us to climb the face of the mountain. I got so angry, thinking to myself, "What does this have to do with learning about God?" The more I looked at the face of the mountain, and remembered my past experience with climbing, the angrier I got. But I did what I was asked to do. The good thing was I had never tried to climb a mountain with the help of a harness and rope before. Even though I slipped and fell backwards, the rope and harness kept me from getting hurt. Finally, I made it to the top. But for some reason I looked down and started to panic. I turned my eyes to the front again and came down the mountain with the help of the rope, the harness, and the anchor person on the ground.

Then, our leaders told us we needed to go back up again, but this time blindfolded. You can imagine my anxiety and anger. How could climbing a mountain blindfolded add to my walk with Christ? But after a few minutes of emotional turmoil, I did what they told me, and started to climb. It was actually easier, since I couldn't see what I was grabbing onto. When my grip or footing slipped, the rope caught me and I would bounce back and keep going. I quickly made it to the top. Actually, I passed the spot I was supposed to reach. Then, I took my blindfold off and looked down, and almost froze. So I put it back on and came down.

It took me a few days to put it all together. In 2 Corinthians 5:7, God says, "We walk by faith, not by sight" (NASB). God was showing me one of the hindrances in serving Him was my faith in my worldly knowledge and experience. Assumptions based on my abilities instead of His were limiting my spiritual growth. My emphasis should've been more on trusting God (the rope) while letting go of worldly sense in exchange for godly sense. I still pray I get better at living this out every day.

At the end of the two years, we were out of money and looking to God for our next step. We knew that whatever direction we took, it needed to be Christ centred. We sent résumés and applications to various ministries. A few times, we came close to getting a job, but a door would always seem to close at the last minute. Then someone at the Bible school put a fax in our mailbox. It was from the director of Teen Challenge Alberta. He was looking for a night person for his treatment centre in Priddis, Alberta. The prospect of working with people in recovery again was not very appealing, but I didn't want to ignore God. So I replied I was interested and the directors sent me plane tickets to Calgary for an interview.

After our meeting, they offered me the position of house supervisor. If I accepted, they would also fix up a place on the grounds where Joyce and I and our children could live. Take my word for it. The place needed a lot of fixing up. I called Joyce and told her I felt God was calling us to Priddis, but the house there was not a palace. Her answer was, "I never asked you for a palace!"

I flew back to Thetis Island. We packed up all our stuff in a rental truck, put our little car behind on a trailer, took two ferries to Vancouver and drove east to Priddis. What a picture! We looked like the Beverly Hillbillies.

We took our time, Joyce being pregnant. Four days later, we got to the grounds of Teen Challenge Alberta. The staff had just completed the renovations on our new accommodation. Some of the staff from Capernwray Harbour had heard about the dirty old red shag carpet in the living room in our future home, and had graciously given us $800 so we could change it. Their concern was for our new child-to-be, who would probably spend most of his time lying or crawling on the carpet. God eventually blessed us with two new boys during our stay at Teen Challenge Alberta. Isaiah came two months after our arrival, and then 18 months later, Isaac.

I had never heard of Teen Challenge before I met the director. As I learned about their program, I could see it was Christ centred. Having never worked in a Christian environment, I believe my expectations were naïve. Most of the staff came from a pool of students who had gone through Teen Challenge and were graduated through the ranks to leadership positions. That created an atmosphere of immature leadership. I seldom sensed a spirit of love from the leadership or the students at the centre. In 1 Timothy 3:6, Paul wrote: "An elder [or leader] must not be a new believer, because he might become proud, and the devil would cause him to fall" (NLT). The fact is all of us wrestle with pride issues, but for a young man who has just graduated from a recovery program, and is too quickly given leadership responsibilities, the result is often tragic.

I had committed to work for Teen Challenge for two years, which I completed. During that time, I saw God work mightily in the areas of answered prayer, financial blessings and two new sons. Although I did not feel very effective at times, I'm still in contact today with some of the students I ministered to.

A few years later as I reflected on my work at the centre, I remember being resentful towards some of the staff because of the lack of love they demonstrated to the students. That's where God came into my thinking and told me, "That's why I put you there, Pierre! The way other staff dealt with the residents is not your concern, but mine."

After resigning from the centre, I was anxious about our future. In a time of prayer, God reminded me to put Him and His Kingdom first and that He would take care of my finances. A few days later, I had lunch with two men who offered to support Joyce and I financially for the rest of the year as we continued to look for God's direction in our lives. This was in May. They offered me $3000 a month for the rest of the year. That was a good day! I've often experienced

God's faithfulness in my life. I sometimes wonder why my faith isn't stronger.

For the first seven or eight months after leaving Teen Challenge, I began developing a recovery ministry. I asked people I respected if they would consider being part of a board of directors to oversee this new ministry. The goal was to provide Christian support for addicts and their families. After about a year, we had counselling services, a 12-Step Christian support group, and an education program for family members. I even tried to train some of the men and women in our ministry who were progressing well as co-facilitators. After a while, we realized the trainees were too young in their recovery. So the board suggested we wait a bit longer before training anyone. I did continue to provide the other services, but after a while it became too much for me to handle. Eventually, I resigned. I had become disillusioned and emotionally tired. I needed to provide for my family, but I needed a change.

I decided to get my Class 1 driver's license and work as a truck driver. After completing my training, I got a job hauling bulk material for a truck company in Calgary. I drove various kinds of tractor-trailers most of the time around town. I did some long haul periodically when there was less work around the Calgary area. It wasn't hard to see God's hand unfolding even when I drove a truck. At various times, I would strike up a conversation with other truck drivers, shippers or receivers. The conversation would result in talking about God. Once I was waiting in line to unload my product, and while talking to another driver who was also waiting to be unloaded, we discussed the need we both felt to experience God more. Another time I was able to lead one of the drivers I worked with to begin a relationship with Jesus Christ. There were many other examples of God's hand going before me, with me, and ahead of me during those few years of driving for a living.

The driving was very hard on my body. It reawakened old spinal injuries. But I needed to continue to work to provide for my family. About 18 months into my new job, I was given a graveyard shift position working from 6 p.m. to 6 a.m., loading and hauling gravel from one end of town to the other. I worked by myself all night in a gravel pit. I would load my truck with a front-end loader and take various types of gravel across town to an asphalt plant to be unloaded.

One evening, as I started my pre-trip on my tractor-trailer, my employer called me into the office and told me I was getting a new partner. To my surprise, he told me it was going to be a woman. Without too much explanation, I told him I wasn't comfortable spending 12 hours alone at night with a woman I didn't know. He was shocked at my response. I told him I would talk to Joyce about it, and if she was okay with it, I would do it. She was. The next evening, the lady started. I could tell right away she didn't have much experience. The next day at the start of the shift, she asked if she could spend the evening in my cab. She told me she lacked experience shifting gears and backing up. She believed if I could train her, this would enhance her skills.

As uncomfortable as that was for me, I allowed her to ride with me that night. Eventually our conversation got around to talking about God. I guess during our talk I shared some of my testimony with her. I told her how my dependency on God instead of myself and drugs had revolutionized my life. Then she made an interesting statement. She said, "When you talk to me about God, I get the same peaceful feelings I had when I was young and my grandmother talked to me about God." I could tell that the Spirit of God was using our conversation to draw her to himself.

The next night, I suggested she drive her own truck. At about 11:30 p.m. at the gravel yard, her truck broke down. I called the mechanic who came down and took a part out of her clutch back to the shop so he could weld it before putting it back. Here we were in the dark at the gravel yard all by ourselves. Needless to say, I felt really uncomfortable. Remembering last night's godly conversation, I asked her if she was interested in hearing about Jesus and God's plan of salvation for the world. She said she was. I then explained the Good News to her and asked if she was interested in receiving Jesus as her Lord and Saviour. She said she was, so I led her in a prayer where she expressed belief in the forgiveness of sin through the blood of Jesus Christ, and a desire to surrender her life to the care and control of the Lord Jesus Christ. Go figure!

In the following weeks, I gave her Christian tapes to listen to. She seemed to get the most from the Bible while listening to it on cassette. At times during a coffee break, I would answer some of the questions she had regarding her walk with Jesus. I could tell by her behaviour and disposition that my decision to obey God in spite of my anxieties had produced fruit. I was looking at a changed person. God is great!

Eventually, the amount of physical discomfort I was experiencing driving a truck grew to a crippling state. I was now experiencing so much burning, cramps and electrical jolts

in my body, I had to stop working as a truck driver.

I decided to go back in ministry helping addicts and their families. I started a counseling service called Immanuel In Recovery.

About a year later, I had an opportunity to come back to Vancouver Island. The Mustard Seed Street Church was opening a healing centre for men whose lives had been affected by a lifestyle of addiction. They were looking for a Christian addiction counsellor to help set up their new facility in Duncan. Joyce and I were excited about the prospect of coming back to British Columbia. After a few interviews, I was offered the position of resident manager at Hope Farm Healing Centre. We lived and ministered at Hope Farm for more than four years.

We experienced God's hand in all areas of our lives and the lives of the people we ministered to. I continued to use the Christian 12-Step material I had used in the past. Together with a Recovery Bible, and a biblical promise book bathed in love and vulnerability, we were able to lead many people to first-time decisions for Christ and baptism. The weak part of the program was the aftercare. Bottom line, we needed more staff to encourage our future disciples to live a clean and sober life and allow the Holy Spirit to change them. It was an exciting and challenging time where Joyce and I grew, especially in the area of community.

For more than 15 years now I have grown in the desire to make available to the 12-Step nation, to Christians in recovery, to church members, to Christian recovery counsellors and groups, and to family members a Christ-centred 12-Step book that would help people know the only true God and His Son, Jesus Christ.

As a former addict who struggled with addictions to alcohol, drugs and promiscuity for many years, I understand the struggles addicts and recovering addicts face. Maybe you're reading this because you're fighting your own addictions. Maybe you know someone who is. I've been through both secular and Christian recovery programs, and have taken what worked for me, and discarded what didn't. What's left is a treatment and recovery program based on solid practices. I am now a certified addiction II counsellor with the Canadian Council of Professional Certification, and an ordained minister with the Canadian Baptists of Western Canada. My prayer is that you will see yourself or a loved one in these pages, and find the help you need to break free. I encourage you to quit and stay quit, work the steps, get a mentor, and live the life Christ has in store for you.

Chapter 4

The Good is Often the Enemy of the Best

W hile He was on earth, Jesus taught His disciples many things. But who did He say he was? Whom did he claim to be? In John 14:6,7, Jesus says, "I am the way, and the truth, and the life; no one comes to the Father but through Me. If you had known Me, you would have known My Father also; from now on you know Him, and have seen Him" (NASB). So who do you say Jesus is?

It's clear Jesus believed He was the Son of God. Was He insane? Not likely. There is too much evidence like fulfillment of prophecy, miracles He performed, His resurrection from the dead, but mostly the millions of testimonies of believers' changed lives. So, if Jesus is right, what about all the other gods that people worship and pray to?

According to Jesus, all other ways to God are deceiving influences from a destructive force or an adversary. This force opposes God's plan for salvation. That force in scriptures is called the evil one, or the Devil. Jesus, talking about the Devil, says, "He was a murderer from the beginning. He has always hated the truth, because there is no truth in him. When he lies, it is consistent with his character; for he is a liar and the father of lies" John 8:44 (NLT).

As someone who struggled with addiction to alcohol, drugs and promiscuity for many years, when I quit drinking and using and worked the 12 Steps, I was moved in Step 3 to make a decision to turn my will and life over to the care of the Father, through His Son, Jesus Christ (the God of my understanding). Bill Wilson, one of the founders of Alcoholics Anonymous, also spoke of this same God of his understanding by calling him "the God of the preachers." In their book *Steps to a New Beginning,* Sam Shoemaker, Dr. Frank Minirth, Dr. Richard Fowler, Dr. Brian Newman and Dave Carter write:

"Many people believe that the 12 Steps began with a small group of recovering alcoholics in the 1930s, men like Bill Wilson and Dr. Bob, the founders of Alcoholics Anonymous, but the truth is that two decades before the 12 Steps were first published in the Big Book of AA, the essential principles of the steps were already being used – not as a vehicle for recovery from addiction, but as a model of authentic Christian commitment, discipleship and witness. Long before they were formulated as the 12 Steps of Alcoholics Anonymous, these principles were at work in the life of a man who would later have a far reaching influence on AA and the entire recovery movement. His name: Sam Shoemaker."

Bill Wilson had many failures at trying to stay sober. When he attended Sam Shoemaker's Calvary Church Mission, he finally gave his life to God. His pride crushed, his defence shattered, Bill had to recognize he was powerless. He had bottomed out. He realized he had to let God take over his life, and when he did, he felt a great peace.

Yet by the late 1930s, Bill Wilson and many other recovering alcoholics in the Oxford Group began to feel the need for a fellowship focused squarely on the problem of alcohol addiction. They wanted a program without religious dogma that welcomed alcoholics of all persuasions, even atheists. Two groups were spun off from the Oxford Group: Alcoholics Anonymous, the prototype of all recovery groups, and Fate at Work, an outreach to lay people. The principles that governed both groups paralleled. By trial and error, the early pre-AA pioneers learned what worked and what didn't in the treatment of their addiction, and then they told the world what they knew.

Even after AA broke away from the Oxford Group, the practices and traditions of the Oxford Group remained the foundation of the AA program and the 12 Steps. The steps themselves are profoundly Christian in character, and each step is rooted in Christian truth. The AA tradition of having people share their stories with the group is a continuation of the Oxford Group practice of sharing testimonies at in-house meetings, which is in turn a continuation of a sharing and witnessing tradition dating back to the 1st-century Church.

One of the most controversial aspects of the 12 Steps is the vague reference to God as "a power greater than ourselves," or "God as we understand Him." Though Sam Shoemaker uncompromisingly preached the Christ of the Bible, he also encouraged spiritual inquirers who didn't believe in Christ to pray to *God* however they perceived Him.

For more than 25 years of being an active member of 12-Step fellowships, I've seen opposition grow to allowing followers of Christ to talk about their higher power. It's subtle, but it's there. People can talk openly about any God of their understanding, but mention Jesus Christ at a meeting, and the atmosphere from those who don't know Him changes instantly.

Jesus says:

"If the world hates you, remember that it hated me first. The world would love you as one of its own if you belonged to it, but you are no longer part of the world. I chose you to come out of the world, so it hates you. Do you remember what I told you? 'A slave is not greater than the master.' Since they persecuted me, naturally they will persecute you. And if they had listened to me, they would listen to you. They will do all this to you because of me, for they have rejected the One who sent me. They would not be guilty if I had not come and spoken to them. But now they have no excuse for their sin. Anyone who hates me also hates my Father" (John 15:18-23, NLT).

I have found it interesting listening to the opposition who says mentioning the word God at meetings might scare the newcomer away or offend the agnostic or atheist. What are they really saying? The feelings of the newcomer or the agnostic need to be given priority over the goals described in AA's Step 12: "Having had a spiritual awakening as a result of these steps, we tried to carry this message to [others]." What message? God loves us and wants to help us find freedom from our addictions. But we need to ask for His help! Bill Wilson and Sam Shoemaker were wrong to resist people who wanted to talk openly at AA meetings about the grace

(the forgiveness and power) of God through his Son Jesus Christ.

Others would say their unwillingness to believe or receive from

Christ stems from the hurt, lying, abuse or hypocrisy they've expe-

rienced at the hands of people who said they were Christians. Let

me suggest that those abusers didn't demonstrate what Jesus is

like. From a logical perspective, it's not a good argument to refuse

God's forgiveness and grace because some Christian didn't behave

the way you think Christians should. There are only two kinds of

people in the world: sinners and sinners that have been forgiven.

Besides, what will you say to God when you meet Him face to face?

Because you will! How do you explain your refusal to the only way

to salvation? Do you say that a so-called Christian misled you, hurt

you and lied to you, so that's why you rejected God's gift?

In John 12:47-48 (NCV), Jesus says, "Anyone who hears my

words and does not obey them, I do not judge, because I did not

come to judge the world, but to save the world. There is a judge for those who refuse to believe in me and do not accept my words. The word I have taught will be their judge on the last day."

The good is often the enemy of the best. I believe that most people in recovery are good people who settle for less. What is the "good" that opposes the "best"? Being clean and sober! What is the best? The abundant life that Jesus promises, and the changes that His Holy Spirit will do in your life when you put your faith in Him.

The Lord's Favour: "But to all who believed [in Jesus] and accepted him [his gift of salvation], he gave the right to become children of God. They are reborn – not with a physical birth resulting from human passion or plan, but a birth that comes from God" (John 1:12-13, NLT).

God loves us! He wants us to experience freedom from guilt, shame and addictions. He wants us to experience the only true God. But it's on His terms, not ours. Come on! Join the adventure! Learn from Jesus, follow His ways, and He will lead you to a challenging and exciting new life.

"No eye has seen, no ear has heard,

and no mind has imagined

what God has prepared

for those who love him."

1 Corinthians 2:9 (NLT)

Chapter 5

The Starting Point

"Don't copy the behavior and customs of this world, but let God transform you into a new person by changing the way you think. Then you will learn to know God's will for you, which is good and pleasing and perfect" (Romans 12:2, NLT).

"As nothing is more easy than to think, so nothing is more difficult than to think well." (Thomas Traherne). If there's a time when we should think well, it should be when we think about God.

What is God like? Does He care about us? Is He a loving God? Christ is the visible image of the invisible God. So if we study Jesus, we'll grow to realize what God is like.

In Luke 15, Jesus uses three parables (stories) to describe God's attitude and character for His flock. They are The Lost Sheep, The Lost Coin, and The Lost Son (or what some people call the Prodigal Son). These three parables demonstrate God's feelings and attitude towards the people He created.

The Lost Sheep (Luke 15:3-7)

Here, God describes himself as a shepherd who is extremely concerned for His lost sheep that has gone astray. When He finds it, after looking for it everywhere, He picks it up, puts it on His shoulders and takes it back to the fold. It's important to see that when the Shepherd finds the sheep, the sheep doesn't resist or try to run away. It doesn't say, "Get away from me! I want to do it my way! I want to find my own way back home!" or "I don't want to go back home." *The sheep submits and surrenders.*

The Lost Coin (Luke 15:8-10)

Here, God describes himself as a woman who, after losing something precious, becomes *determined to find what belongs to her.*

The Lost Son (Luke 15:11-24)

Here, God is pictured as a Jewish father who agrees to divide his wealth between his two sons. A few days later, the younger son leaves for another country with the money.

Left to our imagination is the kind of foolish living he participated in. About the time he runs out of money, there is a great famine. He persuades a local farmer to give him a job –feeding pigs. Not a great job for a Jewish boy. The pay had to be pretty bad since he envied the food the pigs were getting. "No one gave him anything" (no one rescued him). Then, he came to his senses, finally realized what he was doing, and said to himself, "I've made a mess of things. I will humble myself and go back to my father." (He repented).

When he gets back home, we find the father waiting for him, looking for him. The father receives him with open arms and orders his servants to put on him new clothes, shoes, and a ring on his finger signifying whom he belongs to. The father doesn't condemn him. He's just glad to see his son back home again, alive, and wants everyone to rejoice with him.

God's forgiveness, salvation, and abundant life can't be resisted!

Suppose you're the lost sheep. When you see your master coming towards you to rescue you, you run away or refuse to go with him. The salvation of God is not for you at this time. He will not force himself on anyone. The choice to allow yourself to be rescued is yours and yours alone.

If you're the lost son who is just starting out on your journey, arrogant and rebellious, the blessings of God are not for you at this time. If you're the lost son going through a famine (going through hard times) but you don't turn back towards God for help, the blessings of God are not for you at this time. If you're the lost son, overwhelmed weak and miserable, blaming others instead of taking responsibility for your bad choices, the blessings of God are not for you at this time. If you're the lost son who is still trusting in his own abilities, God's blessings are not for you at this time. But, if you're the lost son or daughter who realizes what you have done, accepts the responsibility for your bad choices and turns to God for help in humility, God's mercy and grace *are* for you.

It's true that for most of us, life at times was and is unfair, even terrible. But if we have the courage to look at our past actions, we'll see most of the challenges we've experienced in life had to do with the choices we took. We are born with a streak of self-fixation that wants to control. As we grow in stubbornness and independence, we make choices that sometimes are favourable, and sometimes destructive. There are principles in life that most of us ignore: "You will reap what you sow" and "Choices equal consequences."

So many of us are so busy rebelling and blaming people, places and things, that we don't have the courage to look at the role we played in the life we created for ourselves. The control, the power that everyone has is the power of choice. Every human being is endowed with the choice of how they are going to respond to any situation. They can choose to believe in God or reject Him.

The sooner we realize our need for God, the sooner we'll experience His power in our lives. If we don't, we're left to our own will-power. That is so limited compared to what the Kingdom of heaven has to offer anyone who admits his need for God. We need to turn from false pride and self-reliance.

Others have known the Lord and His blessings in the past, but for some reason decided to do the opposite of what God wants them to do. They are the Jonahs of this world, and are experiencing God's discipline so they can turn back to Him and obey what He has asked them to do. Listen to part of Jonah's story. See if you can relate.

The Story of Jonah (Jonah 1-3, NLT)

Here we have a prophet of God whose job is to pass on God's message to others. God tells him to go to Nineveh and tell the people there to turn from their wicked ways and put their trust in God or He will destroy them and their city. Jonah refuses. He hates the people of Nineveh. They are Israel's enemies. And worse than that, he knows that God is merciful, and there's a possibility after he delivers the message that they may turn from their wicked ways and turn to God and be saved. Jonah doesn't want that, so he refuses. He runs away and takes a boat cruise in the opposite direction. He not only disobeys, he tries to run away from God.

Because of God's love for Jonah and the people in Nineveh, God pursues His prophet. He causes a storm that puts not only Jonah in danger, but all the people around him. Jonah knows the turmoil they're going through is a direct result of his disobedience. The people in the boat don't know that. They sense the storm is part of God's wrath towards somebody in the boat, but to whom? So they pray to their false gods, pleading for mercy.

But the storm gets worse. Eventually, they run into Jonah, who is sleeping downstairs in the ship. They wake him up and tell him to pray to his God so that He will save them. Jonah tells the sailors he knows why they're experiencing this storm. "It's my fault," he says. "I don't want to do what God has called me to do, and that is why we're going through this hell." He does give them the solution to their problem. "Throw me overboard," he says. "Get rid of me, and the storm will stop." At first they refused. They didn't want to have his blood on their hands and be responsible for his death. But the storm got so bad, they changed their minds and threw him overboard. And right away, the storm stopped.

The Sovereign Lord arranged for a big fish to swallow Jonah. Three days later (in the fish), Jonah prayed to the Lord. Imagine what it would be like to be in the belly of a great fish for three days. The acid-like fluids would eat through your skin. The smell would be terrible. You'd be rolling around with other debris, rotten fish and carcasses. No sleep. Some of us can relate. We get the picture. We've experienced similar consequences because of disobedience and attempts to run away from the Lord. Some of us might still be there in the belly of the big fish.

Back to Jonah! By now, he's sorry and crying out to God. Pain is often God's megaphone to get us to change direction. He says, (paraphrasing) "I'm almost dead. Help me, Lord! I can't feel You anymore. You're the only one who can save me." So the Lord got the big fish to throw him up on the beach. Then God said to Jonah a second time, "Go to Nineveh and tell the people there to turn from their wicked ways and turn to Me, or I will destroy them and their city." And this time, Jonah went.

He knew God is merciful and loves all people. He doesn't want anybody to die and go to hell. Jonah knew God is ready to forgive anyone who changes from their sinful ways and turns to Him for salvation. But the Ninevites were Jonah's enemies, the enemies of Israel, and he didn't want to be part of God's plan to save them. Basically, he was pouting and telling God, "I'm not going to do it! I disagree with your plan and I don't want any part of it!"

God hates stubbornness and rebellion. Today in the world, rebellion is often seen as a quality, but in God's eyes, it's the same as someone who worships the Devil. And stubbornness today is often seen as an asset. But in God's Kingdom, it's the same as idolatry. God's blessings are not for the stubborn and rebellious. It's much easier to humble yourself before the Lord now than to have Him create storms in your life so you'll realize your need for obedience. James 4:6 says, "God opposes the proud but gives grace to the humble." Think about it! God *opposes* (pushes against) the proud! But He shows unmerited favour to those who admit their need for Him.

I started this chapter with a quote from Thomas Traherne. If there is ever a time when we should think well, it should be when we think of God. God is love. He values His creation. He declared His plan for our salvation right after the fall of Adam in the Garden of Eden. It continues today, and will continue tomorrow until Jesus returns.

It's a lie to believe all paths lead to heaven. It's foolishness to believe if you perform well enough, God will forgive your sins and allow you to enter heaven when you die. That kind of thinking doesn't line up with the scriptures. Remember, this is not for everyone!

Sadly, there are those God can't help, can't support and can't save. They are the ones who say no to God. God will respect their choice to reject Him. "So God abandoned them to do whatever shameful things their hearts desired. As a result, they did vile and degrading things with each other's bodies. They traded the truth about God for a lie. So they worshiped and served the things God created instead of the Creator himself, who is worthy of eternal praise! Amen (Romans 1:24-25, NLT).

God doesn't need us – we need Him! The worst thing the epitaph on your grave should read: "I did it my way."

Chapter 6

Denial and Addiction

O ne of the greatest supporters of addiction is denial, the power of self-deception, an internal preoccupation with avoiding truth about ourselves and what is happening around us. It's a system of beliefs and behaviours that keeps us from honestly facing our failure to control our drinking, drugging, gambling, sexual behaviour, etc., and the consequences our behaviour has on our relationships with God, others and ourselves.

Why do we lie to ourselves? The simple answer? Fear. We're afraid we may have to stop the behaviour that makes us feel good and more in control. But because of the way denial works, we don't know that. When confronted with our negative behaviour or uncomfortable feelings related to our lust (drinking, using, gambling, overeating, weight control, control of others or various sexual obsessions), we react with behaviours associated with denial like:

- **Minimizing.** "You're exaggerating! It wasn't really that bad!"

- **Blaming.** "It wasn't my fault! Someone else made me do it!"

- **Making excuses.** Also enhances your delusion. "The reason I got drunk was because I drank on an empty stomach."

- **Being hostile.** Here's a great tool that keeps others from sharing their concern about your addictive behaviour.

- **Joking about it.** When others describe last night's embarrassing behaviour as entertaining, it minimizes the seriousness of the situation.

- **Having self-pity.** "Poor me! I had such a difficult childhood, I need to get loaded to help me cope with my past."

- **Withdrawing.** You don't like what's being said to you, so you withdraw mentally or physically.

- **Isolating.** You become a recluse, a closet user or drinker, overeater or sexual deviant, etc.

To continue with your sinful behaviour, you need to minimize your awareness of the consequences your addiction is creating for you and others around you. "Everyone who does evil hates the light, and will not come into the light for fear that his deeds will be exposed" (John 3:20, NIV). This gives power to the evil one, the father of lies, the spirit who works in those who are disobedient.

These symptoms of denial work well. They keep you from realizing that your addictive behaviour is destroying you and your relationships with your significant others. Addiction and denial keep us all from accountability and the possibility of choosing recovery.

You see, when it comes to your habit, you're very protective. When someone said to me, "Pierre, you sure used a lot last night," I'd minimize it. I'd say something like, "That wasn't *that* much for me!" That small statement kept me blinded to the truth that my alcohol and drug use were destructive. Make no mistake: God is right when He says we will reap what we sow!

If our whole lives are centred on one form of drugs or another, our lifestyle will produce a higher degree of unmanageability and powerlessness. As the addiction progresses, there are more and more consequences which affect us, our family, friends, work, finances, etc. This turmoil creates uncomfortable feelings of embarrassment, guilt and shame, inadequacy powerlessness, self-pity and resentment. To suppress those feelings which attacked my pride and self-worth, I unconsciously developed a system of defence that distorted the truth about my behaviour(s), feelings, responsibilities and accountability.

When I started to drink or use drugs, including medication, I discovered it helped me cope with uncomfortable feelings. Sometimes I believed my alcohol and drug use helped medicate the pain caused by childhood trauma. But after years of drinking, using and promiscuity, I became mentally and emotionally sick, which led me to five suicide attempts, psychiatric wards, divorce, work and financial problems. This all fuelled self-pity – probably the most significant tool of denial encouraging drinking and medicating.

Let's not forget our denial support group – people around us who enable us to continue in our addiction. Most don't realize pain is God's megaphone to the addict who still suffers. *Addicts don't often change when they see the light. They change when they feel the heat.* A lot of people who are part of the addict's social network, like family, friends, employers, clergy or co-workers, are easily manipulated to provide support when the addict experiences a crisis. When addicts are using, they're some of the most creative liars around. When dealing with an addict, remember the crisis is a gift. Anyone who wants to help or intervene, including the Christian community, should work at not taking away the consequences which are a direct result of someone's addiction. The exceptions to this rule is if you believe God is asking you to help, or you know the addict has stopped using and they need help to get back on their feet. If possible, don't give them cash. If there are bills to pay, food to buy, equipment or clothes to purchase, be prepared to do it yourself for them. If your desire to control the money meets with too much resistance from the addict, it's probably a scam.

Easier said than done! When it's someone you care about and they're experiencing problems, you want to help. But it's important to weigh the benefits of the help you want to give them. If rescuing them will enable them to continue their lustful behaviour, you need to resist and allow them to reap what they sow. This may cause them to get to the end of themselves (hit rock bottom).

For some, getting to the end of themselves is pretty drastic. We see the love our heavenly Father has for us, shown in the story of The Lost Son. The father, who could intervene at any time, loves the son enough to allow him to get to the end of himself. My senses tell me this loving father would've had a lot of sleepless nights wondering how his boy was doing and wanting him to come home, like any family member would do for someone they cared about.

We need to allow addicted people to hit rock bottom by not supporting their habit in any way, shape or form. Rescuing is not a loving act unless you're sure God is telling you to do it.

Having worked in the jail system for more than six years, I know someone who often ended up in jail due to his behaviours associated with drugs, alcohol and that lifestyle. Many tried to tell him his alcohol and drug use was out of control. Eventually, his family had to disassociate from him to protect themselves. There were divorces, broken relationships, debts owed, violence and physical problems; but none of these consequences seemed to pierce through his walls of self-deception.

During a meeting, he described when he realized he was powerless over his addiction and that his life had become unmanageable. He told of an arrest and conviction. Knowing he would be found guilty and sentenced to jail, he tried to smuggle cocaine into the penitentiary. The idea was to swallow balloons filled with cocaine prior to going in. The balloons act as a protective layer while the cocaine is inside the digestive tract. Then, a day or so later after a bowel movement, the feces are separated from the balloon and the person has successfully brought drugs into the institution. But he didn't know the jail staff were made aware of his plan prior to him entering the jail. Soon after the initial processing, he was placed in segregation with a chamber pot so the staff could monitor his digestive process.

He says he eventually passed the balloons, but as he was sorting through the feces and trying to clean the balloons, he heard the footsteps of a guard approaching, so he spontaneously re-swallowed the balloons so jail officials wouldn't take away his drugs. At that moment, he got to the end of himself. He finally realized to what degree of insane behaviour he was prepared to go to protect his drug of choice, and the amount of control that addiction had over his life. That is where serious recovery began for him.

The experiences that lead people to come to the end of themselves vary – but what *is* important for those who want to help is to not behave in a way that would enable the addict to continue. This only prolongs their life of suffering and denial.

After many years of personal recovery and working with people who struggle with addiction, I know that predisposition may play a role. "You must not have any other god but me. You must not make for yourself an idol of any kind or an image of anything in the heavens or on the earth or in the sea. You must not bow down to them or worship them, for I, the Lord your God, am a jealous God who will not tolerate your affection for any other gods. *I lay the sins of the parents upon their children; the entire family is affected – even children in the third and fourth generations of those who reject me"*(Exodus 20:3-5, NLT).

But we all have choices.

What is addiction? *It's the result of habitually doing what our human nature lusts for in one or more areas of our lives.* We develop an obsessive relationship with something that makes us feel good. If it makes us feel *really* good, we do more of it and more often. If it continues to work well, it becomes an emotional life skill.

As out of control as your addiction has become, the irony is that your addictive behaviour helps you *feel* more in control. You fall in love with the emotional high. You worship it, put your faith in it and become greedy for the experience. You become a slave and even after the high stops working, you continue. When you're compelled or obsessed with the addictive behaviour, you have entered into the later stages of addiction. If you don't stop, you'll give your life for your other god – your addiction.

Recovery or "the new life" must begin with a choice to quit, and stay quit. The Bible talks about turning from your sins and receiving the Good News. But for that to happen, you have to acknowledge your powerlessness, unmanageability and need for God's help. "God blesses those who are poor and realize their need for him, for the Kingdom of Heaven is theirs" (Matthew 5:3, NLT).

Finally, you have to practice honesty about your situation, and your limitations. You have to ask for help and be willing to go to any lengths to quit – and stay quit.

The 12 Steps and How They Work

Step 1: We admit that by ourselves we are powerless to control our addiction(s) and that our lives have become unmanageable.

We admit that we need help!

Step 2: We come to believe that a power greater than ourselves can restore us to sanity.

We begin to hope.

Step 3: We make a decision to turn our will and our lives over to the care of God the Father through His Son, Jesus Christ.

We choose life.

Step 4: We make a searching and fearless moral inventory of ourselves.

We investigate.

Step 5: We admit to God, to ourselves, and to another human being the exact nature of our wrongs.

We confess.

Step 6: We are entirely ready to have God remove all these defects of character.

We repent.

Step 7: We humbly ask Him to remove our shortcomings.

We humble ourselves.

Step 8: We make a list of all persons we have harmed, and become willing to make amends to them all.

We become accountable.

Step 9: We make direct amends to such people wherever possible, except when to do so would injure them or others.

We rebuild relationships.

Step 10: We continue to take personal inventory and when we are wrong, promptly admit it.

We practice accountability.

Step 11: We seek through prayer and meditation to improve our conscious contact with God the Father through His Son, Jesus Christ, praying only for knowledge of His will for us and the power to carry it out.

We seek after Him.

Step 12: Having had a spiritual awakening as a result of these steps, we try to carry this message to other addicts and practise these principles in all our affairs.

We carry the message.

Chapter 7

We Admit That We Need Help!

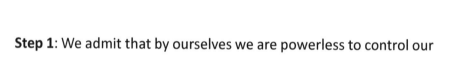

Step 1: We admit that by ourselves we are powerless to control our addiction(s) and that our lives have become unmanageable.

"When I refused to confess my sin, my body wasted away and I groaned all day long. Day and night your hand of discipline was heavy on me. My strength evaporated like water in the summer heat. Finally, I confessed all my sins to you and stopped trying to hide my guilt. I said to myself, 'I will confess my rebellion to the Lord'" (Psalm 32:3-5a, NLT).

The first step is about ownership: "Because of my addictive behaviour(s), my life is a mess and I need help!" Remember: You are as sick as your secrets. To start the healing process, you need to admit there's a problem, and that you can't fix it by yourself.

The 12-Step fellowships encourage their members to practise

HOW:

Honesty – will short-circuit the denial system. Denial is the resistance or refusal to look at your possible addictive behaviour.

Open-mindedness – invites the kind of thinking that challenges addictive thinking. By minimizing your resistance to new ideas and a new way of thinking, you'll have a better chance at success.

Willingness to do what it takes – motivates you to quit and practise staying quit.

What follows is a written exercise that will help you become aware of how much control your behaviour is having on your life.

First, let's look at the mental aspect (addictive thinking):

Give **specific examples** of times when:

❏ You entertained strong thoughts about your addictive behaviour (drinking, using, gambling, pornography etc.)?

_____

_____

_____

_____

❏ You were planning ahead to doing your addictive behaviour?

_____

_____

_____

_____

❏ You were looking forward (anticipating) to doing your addictive behaviour?

_____

_____

_____

☐ You lied about your addictive behaviour?

_____

_____

☐ How many times? 100? 200? 500? 1000? More?

_____

Addictive Behaviour History

Type(s)	Age Started	Age Problematic	Amount	Frequency
e.g. Alcohol	13	18	1 Lt	Daily
e.g. THC	25	28	2 joints	Daily

Now, let's look at your attempts to control the behaviour:

Give **specific examples** of times when:

❒ You tried to cut down:

_____

_____

_____

❒ You tried to quit:

_____

_____

_____

❒ You quit one, but switched to another:

_____

_____

_____

❐ You moved to get away from the consequences of your behaviour:

_____

_____

_____

❐ You went to counselling because of your addictive behaviour:

_____

_____

How many times?

_____

❐ You went to treatment:

_____

_____

How many times?

_____

Affects on school or work?

Because of your addictive behaviour, have you ever:

☐ Shown up for school or work late? **Be specific.**

_____

_____

_____

How often? _____

Because of your addictive behaviour, have you ever:

☐ Been kicked out of or suspended from school?

_____

_____

☐ Been suspended or lost your job? **Be specific.**

_____

_____

❏ Not shown up for work without calling in?

_____

_____

❏ Gotten someone else to phone in sick for you? Who? How

often?

_____

_____

_____

How has your behaviour affected your social life and friends? Give specific examples.

Because of your addictive behaviour, have you:

❏ Isolated more?

❏ Stopped seeing people because they didn't encourage your

behaviour?

❏ Become less active in sports?

❏ Become less active in hobbies?

❏ Become less active in church?

❏ Stopped visiting friend(s)?

❏ Injured others?

What about your values?

❏ List values (things that are important to you) like faithfulness, honesty, loyalty, dependability, kindness, loving, etc.:

_____

_____

_____

❐ Give examples of how you have compromised some of your

values as a result of your behaviours:

_____

_____

_____

❐ Because of your addictive behaviour, have you compromised

your values regarding your sex life or sex roles? **Be specific**.

_____

_____

_____

❐ Is God bringing anything else to your mind right now?

_____

_____

_____

What about your physical health?

How has your addictive behaviour affected you physically?

- ☐ Damage to liver?

- ☐ Lungs?

- ☐ Kidneys?

- ☐ Stomach?

- ☐ Hepatitis?

- ☐ HIV, AIDS?

- ☐ Injuries?

- ☐ Lacerations (Cuts)?

- ☐ Broken bones?

- ☐ Car accidents?

- ☐ Any other?

How has your addictive behaviour affected your finances? Be specific.

☐ Average cost of:

Weekly: _____

Monthly: _____

Yearly: _____

❒ How has your addictive behaviour affected your credit

rating? Please explain.

_____

_____

_____

_____

❒ Can you think of a specific time or times when you spent

money on your behaviour instead of paying bills, alimony,

rent or any other financial responsibility?

_____

_____

_____

_____

☐ Can you think of a situation(s) when you borrowed money to

support your behaviour?

_____

_____

_____

☐ What is the total amount of money you have spent on your

behaviour up to now?

_____

_____

_____

☐ Can you think of any other situations where your behaviour

has affected your finances?

_____

_____

Emotional control

Put check marks beside the feelings you've tried to change or alter:

Shy	Afraid	Frustrated
Guilty	Inadequate	Angry
Ashamed	Defective	Enraged
Bored	Sad	Helpless
Happy	Humiliated	Hurt
Jealous	Lonely	Envious

☐ Any others?

Affects on family and significant others?

Give examples:

☐ Arguing / fighting (physical or verbal abuse)?

_____

_____

_____

_____

☐ Broken promises (grandparents, parents, spouse, children,

friends, etc.)?

_____

_____

_____

_____

☐ Neglecting responsibilities (spouse, children, parents, grand-

parents, in-laws)?

_____

_____

_____

_____

Relationship with God?

Did you ever have one? Yes No

If you did, how has your addictive behaviour affected your ability to:

☐ Love God?

☐ Obey God?

☐ Put God first?

☐ Love others as myself?

Personal Application

1. What are some of the things that stand out from this exercise? **Be specific**.

2. What are you learning personally from the teaching? **Be specific**.

3. What changes do you believe you need to make in response to your new awareness?

4. How can you build into your life the truths in this teaching?

If you realize you *are* addicted, who is to blame? Whose fault is it, anyway? Addiction is caused by *you*, knowingly or unknowingly, surrendering your life to the control of something or someone other than the only true God. You fall in love with it, put your faith in it, worship it, serve it and get greedy for it, becoming a slave to what you've been greedy for. "But each one is tempted when he is carried away and enticed by his own lust. Then when lust has conceived, it gives birth to sin; and when sin is accomplished, it brings forth death" (James 1:14-15, NASB). In your self-focused living, you choose to live life by your own rules – believing yourself to be the centre of the universe, serving in obeying the god of your world – You.

If you're addicted to people, places or things, you need to stop and turn around. The consequences of worshipping other gods –

including yourself – are serious. Don't be misled. Remember, you can't ignore God and get away with it. You will *always* reap what you sow! "Do not be deceived: God cannot be mocked. A man reaps what he sows" (Galations 6:7, NIV).

The solution is to quit and learn how to stay quit. Change direction!

Lustful, greedy behaviour affects your relationship with God and others, and yourself. Recovery is *your* responsibility, and it starts with admitting and accepting you're powerless over your addiction, and that your life has become unmanageable.

Now, you're ready for Step 2.

Preventing Relapse:

What is "preventing relapse"? For now, it's the practice of unselfishness, and shouldering your troubles and responsibilities without the use of mood-altering chemicals or behaviours.

> ➢ Get rid of all paraphernalia that would stimulate your addiction.

> Let go of people who would encourage your addictive behaviour or try to discourage you from moving forward in recovery.

> Don't go to places that would endanger your recovery (if you're addicted to alcohol, don't go sit in a bar!)

"So, my brothers and sisters, we must not be ruled by our sinful selves or live the way our sinful selves want. If you use your lives to do the wrong things your sinful selves want, you will die spiritually. But if you use the Spirit's help to stop doing the wrong things you do with your body, you will have true life" (Romans 8: 12-13, NCV).

Chapter 8

We Begin to Hope

Step 2: We come to believe that a power greater than ourselves can restore us to sanity.

"Ask and it will be given to you; seek and you will find; knock and the door will be opened to you. For everyone who asks receives; he who seeks finds; and to him who knocks, the door will be opened" (Matthew 7:7-8, NIV).

Early in my recovery from addiction to alcohol and other drugs, I chose to go to a treatment facility. I needed help. I couldn't do it on my own. I was afraid that maybe I wouldn't be able to quit and stay quit. I was living on Vancouver Island at the time and the treatment facility was in Vancouver. With a lot of fear and trepidation, I arrived at the recovery centre on a Sunday evening.

The program at the centre taught us new information that challenged our addictive way of thinking The staff encouraged us to express feelings, and to build a social structure that would support our recovery. There was also an introduction to the fellowship of Alcoholics Anonymous. There was group therapy, the object of which was to encourage peer assessment and self-awareness in a somewhat safe environment. That might have been the intention, but the results were different. Maybe because it was too early for many of us in the group, or maybe the counsellors were too aggressive, but the result was that out of 20 people, nine of them left or were asked to leave the centre, suggesting their lack of seriousness about their recovery.

I was so fear based at the time, my mind was having trouble grasping the object of group therapy. I became so afraid of being kicked out, my anxiety level grew.

During one group session, I was told to "shit or get off the pot." I was so confused, I didn't even know I was "on the pot." What I heard was I was going to get kicked out and I didn't even know why.

That night, I had an acute anxiety attack. In desperation, I cried out to God. It had been a long time since I even considered God in dealing with life. Well, go figure! He showed up. I slept well that night, and the next morning I felt strengthened and able to finish the program. That was the beginning of coming to believe for me.

Later that week, I was approached by one of the night supervisors who told me he wanted to have an individual session with me before I left the centre. At first, I was hesitant because I knew this person wanted to talk to me about God. The last time I had talked to a spiritual leader was when I was about 11 or 12 – and he sexually assaulted me.

We had our meeting. I'm not sure what we talked about, but I do remember making a choice to lower my walls of defence and receive the godly information this person was sharing with me. I don't recall exactly what he said, but I do remember feeling a heavy oppression leave my body. Stubbornness and rebellion have no place in the healing process for anyone who struggles with addictions.

You see, after accepting our powerlessness over our addiction and that our lives have become unmanageable, we are left with a void, a helplessness that makes us seek after a power greater than ourselves.

Step 2 is about believing in that greater power that can restore you to sanity. Where does the insanity originate?

- **Addictive thinking.** "I'm addicted to crack, not alcohol,"; "I'm addicted to alcohol, not smoking dope,"; "This time, I'll just have a few"; "I'm not as bad as that person," or some other foolish statement to justify your choices to continue with your obsession. Stupid choices motivated by foolish thinking and the resistance to face the truth about your problem are what encourage insanity in your life. Narcotics Anonymous

(NA) teaches that insanity is repeating the same mistakes over and over again and expecting different results.

- **Dysfunctional emotional life skills**. I learned early in my addictive behaviour that if I was feeling bad, sad or mad, drinking or using would make me feel better. When you habitually allow mood-altering chemicals or behaviours to suppress or accentuate your feelings, you're using an imma-ture emotional life skill. A big part of the insanity is caused by feelings of guilt, shame, helplessness and fear you experi-ence because of your addictive behaviours.

- **Physical insanity** comes by the way you treat your body. The way you eat, sleep or don't sleep, and the various kinds of chemicals you put into your body, as if there were no conse-quences for your actions.

- **Social insanity**. Your whole life and thinking is about your-self. As your obsession progresses, there is no room to think of others, unless to manipulate to get what you need to con-tinue with your addictive behaviour. You deny your responsibilities, accountability, and blame people, places or things for the consequences of your actions.

- **Spiritual insanity**, which flows out of self-centredness. The worst part is you're on your way to hell and don't even know it. You can't be filled or controlled by the Spirit and mood-altering chemicals at the same time. You're either for Christ or against Him. "A thief [Satan] comes to steal and kill and destroy, but I [Jesus] came to give life – life in all its fullness" (John 10:10, NCV). How insane is it to help further the evil one's plan and not even know it?

Coming to believe begins with God. He is like the burning bush that caught the eye of Moses while he was in the desert. However, it was up to Moses to choose to check it out. He could've ignored it, and by doing so missed God's plan for his life. Take a minute to think about what has brought you to this point in your recovery. What were those "God incidents," those favourable coincidences that helped you in your times of need? Be vigilant and keep an open mind. God is with you, and around you.

So how do we start to have faith? Faith comes from hearing about Christ. To attack the mental, emotional, physical, social and spiritual stronghold of insanity, you need to change your addictive thinking with godly thinking. "Do not conform any longer to the pattern of this world, but be transformed by the renewing of your mind. Then you will be able to test and approve what God's will is – his good, pleasing and perfect will" (Romans 12:2, NIV).

Then, you'll come to believe (start to see) that there's a good God out there who loves you, cares for you and wants His best for you. Once you lower the walls of resistance and open yourself up to the possibility God wants to help you, you're working Step 2.

Your concept of God and willingness to act on that concept will influence the quality of your walk with Him. God's Word tells us what God is like. "Christ is the visible image of the invisible God. He existed before God made anything at all and is supreme over all creation. Christ is the one through whom God created everything in heaven and earth. He made the things we can see and the things we can't see – kings, kingdoms, rulers, and authorities. Everything has been created through [Jesus] and for [Jesus]. He existed before everything else began, and he holds all creation together" (Colossians 1:15-17, NLT).

Some think that God is powerful but eager to punish, and that coming to believe in His power can be frightening. The picture we have of God as being only a destructive, unloving force needs to be set aside. We need to invite the possibility that God wants us to succeed so we can get a better picture of what He is like. The key to this step of recovery lies in coming to believe that God's power is a power *for us* rather than *against us*. Remember, He is *Immanuel, God with us*, and wants to lift us out of our depths of despair into His loving presence to discover the life He has planned for us.

Practising Step 2 means choosing to practise believing God is on our side and wants the best for us. "Faith is the confidence that what we hope for will actually happen; it gives us assurance about things we cannot see" (Hebrews 11:1, NLT).

Step 2 is a step of hope! We put our hope in the fact that God is good and that He will help us.

Step 2 Prayer:

> Heavenly Father, forgive me for believing lies about you all these years. I want to know you, the real you. Show yourself to me. Open my eyes for I sincerely seek after you. I, (your name), ask this in Jesus' name, Amen (let it be so).

Preventing Relapse:

- ➤ Don't start your addictive behaviour!

- ➤ Purchase *The Life Recovery Bible*, New Living Translation, by Tyndale publishing. Go to the back of the book and find the Index to 12-Step Devotionals.

- ➤ Begin with Step 1, and then step 2. Read the passages one at a time and personalize them by writing what stands out in the passages – things similar to your life experience up to now. Keep it simple, just a few lines on each passage will do.

In times of trouble, recite and reflect on:

The Serenity Prayer

God, grant me the serenity to accept the things I cannot change;

Courage to change the things I can;

And wisdom to know the difference.

Living one day at a time;

Enjoying one moment at a time;

Accepting hardships as the pathway to peace;

Taking, as the Lord Jesus Christ did, this sinful world as it is,

Not as I would have it.

Trusting that our Lord Jesus will make all things

right if I surrender to His will;

That I may be reasonably happy in this life

and supremely happy with Him forever in the next.

Reinhold Niebuhr

"Do not love the world or the things in the world. If you love the world, the love of the Father is not in you. These are the ways of the world: wanting to please our sinful selves, wanting the sinful things we see, and being too proud of what we have. None of these come from the Father, but all of them come from the world" (I John 2:15-16, NCV).

Chapter 9

We Choose Life

Step 3: We make a decision to turn our will and our lives over to the care of God the Father through His Son, Jesus Christ.

"So humble yourselves under the mighty power of God, and at the right time he will lift you up in honor. Give all your worries and cares to God, for he cares about you" (1 Peter 5:6-7, NLT).

Jesus says, "I am the way, the truth, and the life. No one can come to the Father except through me" (John 14:6, NLT). By now, you may be feeling the tug of God on your life. In Step 1, you saw the results of trying to hold onto the illusion that you were in control. In Step 2, you started to believe there is a God and that He may want to help you. In Step 3, you will make a decision to let go and let God deliver you.

We have all sinned. No one is perfect, except God. And he gave us Jesus, His Son, to pay the ultimate price on the cross for our sins, in our place. How can you be delivered from the old life? The starting point is to become a child of God. This is a decision to believe that Jesus is the Son of God. To receive that He came to earth and gave His life to pay for your sins, and that on the third day, He rose from the grave. This is the most important decision that anyone can make for today and for eternity.

"And this is what God has testified: He has given us eternal life, and this life is in his Son. Whoever has the Son has life; whoever does not have God's Son does not have life. I write this to you who believe in the name of the Son of God, so that you may know you have eternal life" (1 John 5:11-13, NLT).

People who are very analytical have trouble doing Step 3. They complicate the decision-making process by trying to intellectually understand this step before they make a decision. This is just a decision! More will be revealed as we continue to follow Jesus. But this new life won't start until you decide to turn your will and life over to the care and control of God the Father through His Son, Jesus Christ. So what is God like? Study the life of Jesus. That way, you'll get an idea of what God is like. Jesus is the only plumb line in trying to understand God.

In the past, you made decisions to follow other gods. You might not have known it, but you did! From a very young age, we start with "self." Then, it spilled over to other gods like alcohol, drugs, gambling, food or other lustful desires leading to other sinful behaviours, and then to addictions, obsessions and compulsions. You allowed the seduction of euphoric pleasure you got from your behaviour to take over your life, to control your decision-making process which led to insanity and unmanageability. Scripture says there is a way that seems right to us, but this way leads to death.

By sowing those destructive seeds, you allowed your life to be controlled by other idols. From that sinful lifestyle, you reaped feelings of guilt and shame and fear. God sent His Son, Jesus Christ, to rescue you from all those feelings and that old lifestyle – but it's up to you to accept and believe in His gift of salvation.

Step 3 Prayer:

Father God, thank you for sending your Son, Jesus Christ, to suffer and die on a cross to pay the penalty for all my sins. Thank you for raising Him from the dead and giving me an opportunity to receive this new life (His Life) in me. I, (Name), make a decision to surrender all that is in me to the care and control of Jesus Christ, and I accept His gift of abundant life. I choose to trust that His suffering and death on the cross have made me perfect in your eyes. I also choose to believe that after three days He rose from the dead. Dear heavenly Father, fill me with your Holy Spirit. I now ask this in Jesus' name, Amen.

Signed_____

Dated_____

If this is the first time you've received and believed in the Lord Jesus Christ, welcome to the new life. If you're coming back to Him, welcome home!

Preventing Relapse:

➢ Don't start your addictive behaviour!

➢ Don't resurrect the old life in any way, shape or form!

➢ Take time to give thanks to God: morning, lunchtime, evening.

➢ If you haven't done so, look for a church meeting place, one were Christ is preached.

➢ Do Step 3 from the Recovery Bible.

➢ In challenging times, remember the Serenity Prayer.

Chapter 10

We Investigate

Step 4: We make a searching and fearless moral inventory of ourselves.

"Search me, O God, and know my heart; test me and know my anxious thoughts. Point out anything in me that offends you, and lead me along the path of everlasting life" (Psalm 139:23-24, NLT).

Why the inventory? We alcoholics and addicts have a propensity for self- deception, but remember: "Do not be deceived: God cannot be mocked. People reap what they sow" (Galatians 6:7, NIV).

When your addiction has had control over your mind, emotions and spirit, the truth gets distorted. If you're going to succeed in recovery, you need to look at your past behaviours, acknowledge them (Step 5), turn from them (Step 6), and humbly ask God to forgive you and help you change (Step 7).

Why Step 4?

- We need an honest appraisal of ourselves.
- The Lord's searchlight penetrates the human spirit, exposing every hidden motive.

Most of your life has been a life controlled by the addictive mind – the old nature. In your attempts to escape feelings of powerless-ness, guilt, shame, fear, anxiety, hate, anger, resentment, grief and failure, you lived in darkness and didn't even know it.

Your moral life (having to do with right or wrong) has been mostly influenced by the Self Life: self-reliance, self-centredness, selfishness, self-gratification, self-pity and self-indulgence. So, the purpose of doing Step 4 is to sort through the contradiction and confusion in your life regarding morality using God's standards.

Here, you'll make a searching and fearless moral inventory to clarify what right morals are, and help you prepare to admit to God, yourself and to someone else the exact nature of your wrongs.

If you're going to succeed in your recovery, you need to sort through the confusion of godly and ungodly morals. You'll investigate the way you've lived and are living. You'll look at what your Self Life has produced. God's truth will help set you free. Remember Step 3? Remember God's grace, His favour? He will help you. The more we humble ourselves before God and admit our dependence on Him, the more He'll lift us up and give us honour.

By the way, don't confuse doing Step 4 with the problem-solving stages: Step 5 to 7.

> ➤ *Start writing! Why? Unless you write it out, your moral inven-*
> *tory is mostly just theories.*

Let's get started:

- Get a notebook.

- Find a quiet place and turn your phone off.

- Ask for God's help.

- Start writing and don't hold anything back.

- Write about each behaviour, the cause (motive) behind it, and what/who it affected.

Behaviour inventory

The first behaviour to look at is the one that has been eating at you the most.

E.g.:

Behaviour: Cheating on my partner.

Cause behind the behaviour: Self-centredness, lust,
                                                    wanting to please, control.

Who it affected: God, self, spouse and kids.

Now do the same for other behaviours that may apply to you:

Honesty

Lying

Stealing

Cheating

Scheming

Any others?

Pride:

Arrogant

Self-righteous

Unrighteous Anger

Any others?

Jealousy:

Envious

Distrustful

Controlling

Any others?

Lust:

Adultery

Fornication

Pornography

Predatory behaviour

Any others?

Laziness:

Idleness

Inactivity

Procrastination

Any others?

Gluttony:

Drunkenness

Abusing drugs

Abusing food

Any others?

Greed:

Close-fisted (cheap)

Love of money

Gambling

Any others?

Resentment inventory: obsessive hostility towards others.

Resentment	the cause	the effect	my part
e.g.: Father	didn't love me enough	lack of respect	unforgiveness

Resentment	the cause	the effect	my part

Relationship resentments

God

Family (old and new)

Friends

Neighbours

Enemies

Any others?

Institution resentments

Work

School

Church

Anyone or anything else?

"But you [God] desire honesty from the heart, so you can teach me to be wise in my inmost being" (Psalm 51:6, NIV)

Preventing Relapse:

- ➤ Don't start your addictive behaviour!
- ➤ Don't resurrect the old life in any way, shape or form!
- ➤ Take time to give thanks to God: morning, lunchtime, evening.
- ➤ Find someone to do your step 5 with and do your step 5.
- ➤ Do Step 4 from the Recovery Bible.
- ➤ In challenging times, remember the Serenity Prayer.

Chapter 11

We Confess

Step 5: We admit to God, to ourselves, and to another human being the exact nature of our wrongs.

"Confess your sins to each other and pray for each other so that you may be healed. The earnest prayer of a righteous person has great power and wonderful results" (James 5:16, NLT).

J ust like in Step 1, where admitting your powerlessness and unmanageability was a necessity in moving forward, admitting to God, to yourself and to someone else in Step 5 is also an important step for continuous spiritual growth in your recovery.

Persevere! God Is with You Always

"Be strong and courageous, and do the work. Don't be afraid or discouraged [by the size of the task], for the Lord God, my God, is with you. He will not fail you or forsake you. He will see to it that all the work related to the Temple of the Lord is finished correctly" (I Chronicles 28:20, NLT). You are the temple of His Holy Spirit if you have the Lord Jesus Christ as your Saviour.

Admit to God. **Why?**

If you say you have no sin, you're only fooling yourself and refusing to accept the truth. When you confess your sins to the Lord, He forgives you, and the slate is wiped clean.

Admit to ourselves. **Why?**

As you write your inventory, you'll see your behaviours for what they really are. In Step 5, you consciously admit your wrongs. You *accept the responsibility* for what you've done.

Admit to another person. **Why?**

Telling your story to another person may cause you added fear. However, it's essential that with God's help you disclose your true nature with an other Christian so he/she can pray for you to be healed. Until you sit down and talk about what you've been hiding and carrying around for such a long time, your house cleaning is mostly theoretical. The loving support of another person may help you clarify patterns that trigger or fuel your sinful, addictive nature.

When?

You need to continue with Step 5 soon after finishing Step 4. If you wait, your defences may resurface. You might justifiy, minimize, rationalize, procrastinate or project (blame others). When this happens, you give power back to the evil one who doesn't want you to be set free. He wants to keep you in bondage for himself.

With whom do we do it?

A mature Christian, preferably of the same sex, like a pastor, counsellor, priest, nun, etc. What is important is that you find someone with whom you feel somewhat safe.

So, admit the exact nature of your wrongs, do it soon after completing Step 4, and do it with someone safe. Read all of it, and let it go. Now you're ready for Steps 6 and 7.

Preventing Relapse:

➢ Don't start your addictive behaviour!

➢ Don't resurrect the old life in any way, shape or form!

➢ Take time to give thanks to God: morning, lunchtime, evening.

➢ Do Step 5 from the Recovery Bible.

➢ In challenging times, remember the Serenity Prayer.

Chapter 12

We Repent

Step 6: We are entirely ready to have God remove all these defects of character.

"Blessed are those who hunger and thirst for righteousness, for they will be filled" (Matthew 5:6, NIV).

Surrender! You have proven that with your own strength, abilities and self-centred motives, you're unable to become what God wants you to be. The call to repentance on the part of man is a call for him/her to change direction from ungodly dependencies to becoming completely dependent on God. We don't come to God

on our own terms, but on His. Jesus says, "The time has come ...
the kingdom of God has come near. Repent and believe the good
news!" (Mark 1:15, NIV). Repentance (changing direction) is both a
privilege and an opportunity.

What leads people to repentance?

☐ Conviction of ungodly behaviour.

☐ God's kindness and patience.

What do I repent (turn) from?

☐ The world's sin is that it refuses to believe in Jesus.

☐ Sins motivated by the self-life:

Sins:	Greed	Bursts of anger
	Lust	Disputes
	Evil desires	Dissension
	Sexual immorality	Faction
	Impurity	Envy

Sensuality	Drunkenness
Idolatry	Revelling
Sorcery	Dishonesty
Hatred	Stealing
Strife	Blasphemy
Jealousy	Foul speech or swearing
Dishonouring your parents	

How do I repent?

Stop. Abstain. Turn from and put to death. Change your thinking about the ungodly way you're behaving. And if you don't?

"He has been very kind and patient, waiting for you to change, but you think nothing of his kindness. Perhaps you do not understand that God is kind to you so you will change your hearts and lives. But you are stubborn and refuse to change, so you are making your own punishment even greater on the day he shows his anger. On that day everyone will see God's right judgments. God will reward or punish every person for what that person has done. Some people, by always continuing to do good, live for God's glory, for honor, and for life that has no end. God will give them life forever. But other people are selfish. They refuse to follow truth and, instead, follow evil. God will give them his punishment and anger. He will give trouble and suffering to everyone who does evil – to the Jews first and also to those who are not Jews. But he will give glory, honor, and peace to everyone who does good – to the Jews first and also to those who are not Jews. For God judges all people in the same way" (Romans 2:4-11, NCV).

You may say, "There are too many things I need to change. How can I do all this?" In your own strength, you can't! But God can. You can do all things through Him. This is where Step 7 comes in.

Preventing Relapse:

> ➤ Don't start your addictive behaviour!

> ➤ Don't resurrect the old life in any way, shape or form!

➤ Take time to give thanks to God: morning, lunchtime, evening.

➤ Do Step 6 from the Recovery Bible.

➤ In challenging times, remember the Serenity Prayer.

Chapter 13

We Humble Ourselves

Step 7: We humbly ask Him to remove our shortcomings.

"But if we confess our sins to him, he is faithful and just to forgive us and to cleanse us from every wrong" (I John 1:9, NLT).

So you've completed Step 5 by admitting to God, yourself, and to another human being the exact nature of your wrongs. You have confessed! And at this moment you're entirely ready to turn from your old ways of self-reliance and selfishness, and want God to change you because you can't do it on your own. You're ready to ask God to remove all your shortcomings.

If you're at Step 7, as a follower of Jesus Christ, you've received the forgiveness of God for all your sins. We believe "it was our weaknesses [Jesus] carried; it was our sorrows that weighed him down. And we thought his troubles were a punishment from God, a punishment for his own sins! But [Jesus] was pierced for our rebellion, crushed for our sins. He was beaten so we could be whole. He was whipped so we could be healed. All of us, like sheep, have strayed away. We have left God's paths to follow our own. Yet the Lord laid on [Jesus] the sins of us all" (Isaiah 53:4-6, NLT).

So as far as God's judgement is concerned, Jesus has taken care of that. But what about behaviour modification? Sinful behaviours you'd like to change. How do you do that?

There are a few people I've met over the years that had a "Damascus" experience – a complete change in behaviours and attitudes. A friend of mine not only received the forgiveness of sins through faith in Jesus Christ, but was drastically changed. He stopped smoking and swearing, his obsession with using drugs and alcohol completely disappeared. His love for his fellow human beings grew, and so did his desire to tell others about Jesus. Instant, dramatic changes.

But for most of us, we're grateful to receive the forgiveness for all our sins. We're motivated by the Holy Spirit to put our trust in Jesus, and we experience the disappearance of some of our short-comings – but it's a long way from a complete change of thinking and attitude.

So how do you live out the Christian life? How do you experience the changes that need to happen in the life of a follower of Christ? God calls us to accept the death of the old life (man) and equally calls us to put on the new life (Christ).

We need to change the way we think because Jesus tells us, "It is what comes from inside that defiles you. For from within, out of a person's heart, come evil thoughts, sexual immorality, theft, murder, adultery, greed, wickedness, deceit, lustful desires, envy, slander, pride, and foolishness. All these vile things come from within; they are what defile you" (Mark 7:20-23, NLT) and make you unacceptable to God. "Instead, there must be a spiritual renewal of your thoughts and attitude" (Ephesians 4:23, NLT).

We are called to give our bodies, minds and behaviours over to God, and to listen to His Word, allowing Him to renew our thinking and find His will for our lives. Don't focus on your sins. Focus on God's forgiveness. Humble yourself and ask for His help to change.

"So, my brothers and sisters, we must not be ruled by our sinful selves or live the way our sinful selves want. If you use your lives to do the wrong things your sinful selves want, you will die spiritually. But if you use the Spirit's help to stop doing the wrong things you do with your body, you will have true life" (Romans 8:12-13, NCV).

What do we entertain in our hearts? What do we say?

Step 7 Prayer:

"Heavenly Father, I, <u>Name</u>, *humble* myself before you. Without you, I can do nothing. I'm willing and ready to have you remove all my shortcomings, defects and sins.

I surrender all of me. Take away everything that stops me from having a more loving and enjoyable relationship with you and with others. I ask this in the name of my Lord and Saviour, Jesus Christ, Amen."

Humility is the key. To grow in the understanding of who God is and who you are apart from Him. God can do great things with his humble follower.

It's impossible to put on a new identity while holding onto the old one. Remember, you reap what you sow. If you don't allow pride to control your life, but practice humility instead, you will experience His abundant life.

Preventing Relapse:

> ➤ Don't start your addictive behaviour!

> ➤ Don't resurrect the old life in any way, shape or form!

> ➤ Take time to give thanks to God: morning, lunchtime, evening.

> ➤ Practice humility in your prayers.

> ➤ Practice allowing others to get the glory instead of you.

> ➤ Do step 7 in the Recovery Bible

> ➤ In challenging times, remember the Serenity Prayer.

Chapter 14

We Become Accountable

Step 8: We make a list of all persons we have harmed, and become willing to make amends to them all.

"Turn away from evil and do good. Work hard at living at peace with others" (1 Peter 3:11, NLT).

I would like to inspire you to work very hard on Steps 8 and 9. Often, people will do a great job at working their program until they come to these two steps. The fear of following through, for some, is often motivated by the fear of rejection or lack of humility needed to be successful. As someone who has worked the steps and experienced the benefits of making a list and making amends wherever possible, I would encourage you to persevere and follow through. The result will be a sense of freedom like you have never experience before.

Let me take you back to your childhood. Maybe you stole something. Maybe it was money from your parents, a grandparent, uncle or aunt. Maybe it was from a store, a restaurant, church, etc. You get the picture. Then, because of the guilt, you admitted to it, made amends/restitution. Remember the relief you felt after? That's what I want for you. More importantly, it's what God wants for you.

Some of us know that God is a forgiving God, but I also want you to consider that people, especially those who care about us, are also very forgiving. The majority of them didn't leave us – we left them. We're the ones who abused the relationships. These steps are a great place to start rebuilding those relationships, and it begins by making a list of all the people you've harmed, and becoming willing to make amends to them all.

Something else to consider: God tells us in His Word our reluctance to start that process affects our worship and requests to God. First things first! "So if you are presenting a sacrifice at the altar in the Temple *and you suddenly remember that someone has something against you*, leave your sacrifice there at the altar. Go and be reconciled to that person. Then come and offer your sacrifice to God" (Matthew 5:23-24, NLT).

Where do you start? Make a list. To continue clearing away the wreckage of your past, you need to sort out who it is you need to make amends to. At this point, focus only on Step 8 (making the list). Don't worry about Step 9 (making amends). That comes later.

With the list, it's important to be specific. Ask the Spirit of God to reveal to you who He wants you to put on the list. Step away from justification, rationalization or self-pity in doing these steps. When resistance to working the steps shows its ugly face, pray this prayer. I believe it originated with St. Augustine, and it was passed on to me by Pastor Mark Buchanan in a time of change in my life: "Lord, deliver me from this lust of always vindicating myself!" It's true your addiction played a part in initiating your wrongdoing. Big deal! You're still responsible for your actions.

Just start. Review Step 4 and start putting down the names of people you've harmed. Write down *who and how* you harmed those people. Whenever you're unsure if you should or shouldn't put a person on your list, ask yourself, "Have I wronged this person in any way?" If the answer is yes, then *become willing* to make amends. It's a choice. You need to do this to

move forward in rebuilding your relationships, but most of all because God wants you to.

While making the list, look at your responsibility, not the person you harmed. God wants you to pursue peace, to work hard at loving others. Your resentment towards them affects your spiritual growth and could lead you to relapse. From the experiences of those who have failed in recovery, we learn that we can bury our list in a drawer, but we can't bury the guilt, remorse and resentment we feel for very long without returning to active addiction.

"Don't let evil conquer you, but conquer evil by doing good" (Romans 12:21, NLT).

Who do you put on the list?

Family?

Friends?

Employers?

Deceased relationships?

Enemies?

Creditors?

Anyone else who doesn't fall into the above categories and has been harmed because of your poor choices?

On your list, write:

- ➢ Whom did I hurt?

- ➢ How did I hurt them?

- ➢ Will it make things worse for them if I make amends?

- ➢ Will it harm someone else?

Then become willing to make amends to them all.

Preventing Relapse:

➢ Write your Step 8 lists.

➢ Don't start your addictive behaviour!

➢ Don't resurrect the old life in any way, shape or form!

➢ Take time to give thanks to God: morning, lunchtime, evening.

➢ Practice humility in your prayers.

➢ Practice allowing others to get the glory instead of you.

➢ Do step 8 in the Recovery Bible

➢ In challenging times, remember the Serenity Prayer.

Chapter 15

We Rebuild Relationships

Step 9: We make direct amends to such people wherever possible, except when to do so would injure them or others.

"Do your part to live in peace with everyone, as much as possible" (Romans 12:18, NLT).

B e a peacemaker. Take the first step! "God blesses those who work for peace, for they will be called the children of God" (Matthew 5:9, NLT). Remember, there is a God equation in everything. He opposes the proud *but gives grace* to the humble. He is with you!

We make direct amends. Contact the person and admit the degree of your wrongs, and ask for forgiveness. Accepting responsibility for the harm done can be an awkward experience (humbling) as it forces you to admit the affect you've had on others. But you need to do it if you want to be successful in working this step.

To such people wherever possible. How? Make a plan. Take a name from your Step 8 list. Contact them and ask them if and when there would be a convenient time for you to get together. Put yourself at their disposal (humble yourself). Then, when you're with this person, get their attention and ask for forgiveness for the wrongs you have done to them.

Other times, just make amends whenever the opportunity presents itself. This is less planned and more spontaneous. Look at those opportune times as God incidents. There will be some situations, some wrongs that can never be fully repaired. You need to accept this. Also sometimes you might have forgotten the person's name you harmed, or it has been such a long time since your last contact with them, you wouldn't have a clue where to start looking.

In those times, willingness to make amends can serve in the place of action.

Except when to do so would injure them or others. You need to evaluate each situation to see if making amends would cause even more pain to the person. Some questions you may want to ask yourself first: Will it make things worse for them? Will it harm someone else? If the answer is yes to any of those questions, don't be selfish. Move on to the next name.

If someone on your list has died and you feel there was some unfinished business between you, some people have found that writing out their amends on a piece of paper and reading it out loud to God helps them deal with the guilt and shame they feel because of their behaviour.

Remember:

"But he [Jesus] took our suffering on him and felt our pain for us. We saw his suffering and thought God was punishing him. But he was wounded for the wrong we did; he was crushed for the evil we did. The punishment, which made us well, was given to him, and we are healed because of his wounds" (Isaiah 53:4-5, NCV).

Good judgement, a good sense of timing, and courage are assets that will help you to be successful in doing your Step 9. Making amends will release you from feelings of guilt, shame and fear, and will replace them with a serenity of relief and peace.

Step 9 Prayer

Dear Father God,

Thank you for your love, for your helpful grace. Help me model your ways when I make amends to those I have hurt, and offer forgiveness to those who have injured me.

I humble myself and set aside my selfishness and pride. I pray you would help me focus only on my part and my responsibilities while I make amends. Please put your healing hands on the people that I have hurt, and on the people who have hurt me. Thank you for forgiving me and help me to forgive others.

In Jesus' name I pray, Amen.

Preventing Relapse:

➢ Make amends!

➢ Don't start your addictive behaviour!

➢ Don't resurrect the old life in any way, shape or form!

➤ Take time to give thanks to God: morning, lunchtime, evening.

➤ Practice humility in your prayers and with others.

➤ Allow others to get the glory.

➤ Do step 9 in the Recovery Bible

➤ In challenging times, remember the Serenity Prayer.

Chapter 16

We Practise Accountability

Step 10: We continue to take personal inventory and when we are wrong, promptly admit it.

"Try to live in peace with everyone and seek to live a clean and holy life, for those who are not holy will not see the Lord" (Hebrews 12:14, NLT).

To the best of your ability, you've dealt with the wreckage of your past by working the preceding nine steps. Step 10 helps you deal with the wreckage of the present. It's just good sense to not let things build up in your life. When you allow unattended responsibilities to accumulate, they create stress. Often, you're unaware of the progressive stress accumulating through your daily emotional baggage of guilt, anger and resentment. That is why a daily personal inventory is helpful and effective in dealing with the challenges of the day. You need to clean your "space." You need to assess your day and determine if change is needed to protect your relationship with God, others and with yourself.

We continue to take personal inventory. Continue the process of humble self-appraisal.

And when we are wrong, promptly admit it. When you're not sure if an amend needs to be made, ask God to help you see clearly. Did you cause harm? Do you need to make it right? If the answer is yes, grow up, accept the responsibility, admit your part and do it quickly. By now, you should know how to do this. You need to continue obeying God by loving God and loving your neighbour as yourself.

Let's look at the different types of inventory you can do during the day. Think HALT. Periodically, when you feel overwhelmed, ask yourself: Am I too **H**ungry? Too **A**ngry? Too **L**onely? Too **T**ired? If the answer is yes to any of these, you need to stop what you're doing, and make better choices before those feelings influence you away from recovery. *If you're hungry, you need to eat something. If you're angry, you need to forgive someone. If you're lonely, you need to call someone. And if you're tired, you need to rest.* If you don't take care of those challenges, they will take care of you, and not in a positive way.

Then there is the evening inventory, maybe just before bed-time. Ask: "How's my relationship with God? How's my relationship with others? How's my relationship with myself? Do I need to confess something to God? Do I need to make amends to someone?" If there are amends to be made, the next day look for an opportunity to do it. Don't procrastinate. Deal with it ASAP. and move on. "Am I taking care of myself?" If not, you need to make it a priority so you can function better.

Look back and see how far you've come by admitting mistakes, trusting and obeying God, and working the steps. Continue to renew your mind with God's Word and what He wants for your life. Stay alert. We all have a tendency to be self-deceived. A daily inventory helps to minimize denial and encourages truth.

Remember: "A prudent person foresees the danger ahead and takes precautions. The simpleton goes blindly on and suffers the consequences" (Proverbs 27:12, NLT).

Every day, ask yourself: Did I love God the most today? Did I love my neighbour as myself? Am I taking good care of myself? *Allow God to continue His work in you and through you.*

Don't lose track of what lies ahead: "Brothers [and sisters], I do not consider myself yet to have taken hold of it. But one thing I do: Forgetting what is behind and straining toward what is ahead, I press on towards the goal to win the prize for which God has called me heavenward in Christ Jesus" (Philippians 3:13-14, NIV).

Amen!

Preventing Relapse:

- ➤ Every day, do a Step 10 inventory.

- ➤ Don't start your addictive behaviour!

- ➤ Don't resurrect the old life in any way, shape or form!

- ➤ Take time to give thanks to God: morning, lunchtime, evening.

- ➤ Practice humility in your prayers and with others.

- ➤ Allow others to get the glory.

- ➤ Do step 10 in the Recovery Bible

- ➤ In challenging times, remember the Serenity Prayer.

Chapter 17

We Seek After Him

Step 11: We seek through prayer and meditation to improve our conscious contact with God the Father through His Son, Jesus Christ, praying only for knowledge of His will for us and the power to carry it out.

"So brothers and sisters, since God has shown us great mercy, I beg you to offer your lives as a living sacrifice to him. Your offering must be only for God and pleasing to him, which is the spiritual way for you to worship. Do not change yourselves to be like the people of this world, but be changed within by a new way of thinking. Then you will be able to decide what God wants for you; you will know what is good and pleasing to him and what is perfect" (Romans 12:1-2, NCV).

S tep 11 is about drawing closer to God and seeking after Him. We want to know Him more, and to be empowered by Him to do His will.

We seek through prayer. "And now about prayer. When you pray, don't be like the hypocrites who love to pray publicly on street corners and in the synagogues where everyone can see them. I assure you, that is all the reward they will ever get.

But when you pray, go away by yourself, shut the door behind you, and pray to your Father secretly. Then your Father, who knows all secrets, will reward you. When you pray, don't babble on and on as people of other religions do. They think their prayers are answered only by repeating their words again and again. Don't be like them, because your Father knows exactly what you need even before you ask him! Pray like this:

Our Father in heaven,

May your name be honored.

May your Kingdom come soon.

May your will be done here on earth,

Just as it is in heaven.

Give us our food for today,

And forgive us our sins,

Just as we have forgiven

Those who have sinned against us.

And don't let us yield to temptation,

But deliver us from the evil one " (Matthew 6:5-13, NLT).

This blueprint for prayer that Jesus left us encourages us to first talk to God about our desire to see Him glorified, and for His will to dominate the earth just like it dominates the heavens.

Secondly, Jesus encourages us to bring to the Father our needs of the day for food, for His gracious forgiveness, direction and protection. And just as Jesus has forgiven our sins, we're told to forgive others.

And meditation. What is meditation? It's contemplating, considering carefully. To put our full attention on something. What are we as Christians to contemplate? What arc we luld to consider carefully in the mind. Here are some ideas of what a follower of Christ could meditate on:

1. The person of God. Do you know how we get to know God better? We look to Jesus.

2. God's words. "Study this Book of Instruction continually. Meditate on it day and night so you will be sure to obey everything written in it. Only then will you prosper and succeed in all you do" (Joshua 1:8, NLT).
"I have hidden your word in my heart that I might not sin against you. (Psalm 119:11, NIV).

3. His Works. Ask God to reveal himself to you in His work. "For the truth about God is known to them instinctively. God has put this knowledge in their hearts. From the time the world was created, people have seen the earth and sky and all that God made. They can clearly see His invisible qualities – His eternal power and divine nature" (Romans 1:19-20, NLT).

I remember early in recovery, I was around people who talked about experiencing God in nature. I used to get so frustrated because I didn't get it. I complained to God, asking Him to show him-self to me in His creation. At the time I was at Capernwray Harbour Bible School as a student. That afternoon, my job was to work in the garden cutting down old flowers and digging up old bulbs so they could be replanted the following year at the proper time.

Suddenly, I realized this represented (imperfect as it may be) a representation of the death, burial and resurrection of Jesus Christ. Cutting down the plants represented Jesus' death on the cross. Digging up and putting away the old bulbs represented His burial, and the following spring, that bulb would be replanted and a new, beautiful flower would grow again. I was amazed! He is amazing! If you're not sure how to do it, ask Him to help you see with new eyes His creation all around you. Always invite God into the process. Better yet, realize He is with you always.

An old Christian teaching on meditation suggests reading a short passage of scripture slowly about 5-10 times, and then thinking about what the Holy Spirit of God is showing you. What is He saying to you personally? What stands out from the passage? Sometimes it's a word, a sentence, a new awareness, etc. Let me encourage you to write that stuff down because "God is speaking" to you personally.

So what do you seek through prayer and meditation?

To improve your conscious contact with God the Father through Jesus Christ. Always make sure nothing is impeding your prayer, like resentment or unforgiveness.

Through prayer and meditation, you'll progress in your understanding of Him, His ways and His works. The more you study Jesus, His teachings, His character, the more you'll understand the Father and His amazing love for you and others.

Praying only for knowledge of His will for us. How do you find out about His will? If your thinking or will lines up with scriptures, then it's probably God's will for your life! The more familiar you are with scriptures, the better you can discern what is God's will. For example, the world says: "God helps those who help themselves" But the scriptures say, "Blessed are the (*people who know they are*) poor in spirit, for theirs is the Kingdom of heaven." (Matthew 5:6, NASB)

Am I helping (ministering) in some way with other believers in furthering the Kingdom of God? This is God's will for His children! And how do we do all this? How do we find the power to carry it out? We practice remembering the power of God, Jesus' Spirit is with us, and lives in us.

"This message is the secret that was hidden from everyone since the beginning of time, but now it is made known to God's holy people. God decided to let his people know this rich and glorious secret which he has for all people. *This secret is Christ himself, who is in you*. He is our only hope for glory. So we continue to preach Christ to each person, using all wisdom to warn and to teach everyone, in order to bring each one into God's presence as a mature person in Christ. To do this, I work and struggle, using Christ's great strength that works so powerfully in me" (Colossians 1:26-29, NCV).

I feel I would be delinquent in my responsibilities if I didn't talk about the importance of worship as a huge part of God's will for our lives. There are discussions, arguments, and books written on how to worship. Consider the simplicity of worship I heard from my pastor, Mark Buchanan, during a Sunday service at New Life Baptist Church in Duncan. He described worship as complete attention, adoration and surrender to God. I don't know about you, but I know that I'm mostly self-focused during my time of singing and praying. If we were to practice this change of focus during our church meeting times, we would grow in leaps and bounds in our walk with God.

Focus less on our kingdom, our will, our wants, ourselves. Become more God centered, praying only for His will, His Kingdom and the ability to love Him the most and love others as ourselves. The more we become concerned about building His Kingdom, doing His will and obeying His commandments, the more we experience His power to carry it out.

Preventing Relapse:

> ➤ Learn to focus on God instead of yourself.

> ➤ Don't start your addictive behaviour!

> ➤ Don't resurrect the old life in any way, shape or form!

> ➤ Take time to give thanks to God: morning, lunchtime, evening.

> ➤ Practice humility in your prayers and with others.

> ➤ Allow others to get the glory.

> ➤ Get involved with your church community.

> ➤ Do step 11 in the Recovery Bible

> ➤ In challenging times, remember the Serenity Prayer.

Chapter 18

We Carry the Message

Step 12: Having had a spiritual awakening as a result of these steps, we try to carry this message to other addicts and practice these principles in all our affairs.

"All praise to the God and Father of our Lord Jesus Christ. He is the source of every mercy and the God who comforts us. He comforts us in all our troubles so that we can comfort others. When others are troubled, we will be able to give them the same comfort God has given us" (2 Corinthians 1:3-4, NLT).

Having had a spiritual awakening. There is a difference here between AA's Step 12 and a Christian way of looking at how we get our spiritual awakening. As Christians, we know it's the Holy Spirit that awakens *our* spirit when we put our trust in Jesus Christ for our salvation and for the abundant life that He promises. It's by believing in Jesus and receiving His saving work on the cross for us that we receive our spiritual awakening. We're reborn and this rebirth is from God.

"God saved you by his special favor when you believed. And you can't take credit for this; it is a gift from God. Salvation is not a reward for the good things we have done, so none of us can boast about it. For we are God's masterpiece, *He has created us anew in Christ Jesus*, so that we can do the good things he planned for us long ago" (Ephesians 2:8-10, NLT).

We try to carry this message to other addicts. In AA, they say, "We can only keep what we have by giving it away." Here are some guidelines that will be helpful as you continue to carry the message of God's grace to the addict who still suffers:

1. Before every situation, remember that God is with you. He is your helper. Pray for the person you're going to see.

2. When called to help others, try to find out as much as you can before going.

3. In your conversation with the addict, share that your problem was not only quitting, but staying quit.

4. Keep the advice to a minimum. Share mostly what your decision to believe and receive the Good News has done for you.

5. If you're meeting with a person of the opposite sex, don't go to their house by yourself. Find a public place to talk to them, like a restaurant or coffee place.

6. Always try to go with another person. If you can't find someone else, use wisdom. Don't set yourself up to relapse. "Dear brothers and sisters, if another Christian is overcome by some sin, you who are godly should gently and humbly help that person back onto the right path. And be careful not to fall into the same temptation yourself" (Galatians 6:1, NLT).

And remember what scripture says about dealing with difficult people – and some of the people we deal with are difficult. "Don't get involved in foolish, ignorant arguments that only start fights. The Lord's servants must not quarrel but must be kind to everyone. They must be able to teach effectively and be patient with difficult people. They should gently teach those who oppose the truth. *Perhaps God will change those people's hearts* and they will believe the truth. Then they will come to their senses and escape from the Devil's trap. For they have been held captive by him to do whatever he wants" (II Timothy 2:23-26, NLT).

Key attitudes in carrying the message

Love   -   Compassion   -   Respect

And practice these principles in all our affairs. How? Let's review the steps.

Step 1: We admit that by ourselves we are powerless to control our addiction(s) and that our lives have become unmanageable.

We accept the responsibility for our addiction and our need for help!

* * *

Step 2: We come to believe that a power greater than ourselves can restore us to sanity.

We choose to believe that God exists and that He wants to help us!

* * *

Step 3: We make a decision to turn our will and our lives over to the care of God the Father through His Son, Jesus Christ.

We let go and let God!

* * *

Step 4: We make a searching and fearless moral inventory of ourselves.

We write a complete moral inventory of our life.

* * *

Step 5: We admit to God, to ourselves, and to another human being the exact nature of our wrongs.

We agree with God we are reaping what we have sown!

* * *

Step 6: We are entirely ready to have God remove all these defects of character.

We want God's forgiveness and help to change.

* * *

Step 7: We humbly ask Him to remove our shortcomings.

<u>We humbly ask for God's mercy and grace.</u>

*   *   *

Step 8: We make a list of all persons we have harmed, and become willing to make amends to them all.

<u>We prepare to rebuild our relationships.</u>

*   *   *

Step 9: We make direct amends to such people wherever possible, except when to do so would injure them or others.

<u>We rebuild!</u>

*   *   *

Step 10: We continue to take personal inventory and when we are wrong, promptly admit it.

We review our day and learn from our mistakes.

*　*　*

Step 11: We seek through prayer and meditation to improve our conscious contact with God the Father through His Son, Jesus Christ, praying only for knowledge of His will for us and the power to carry it out.

We pursue intimacy with God, and join in His plan for our lives.

*　*　*

Step 12: Having had a spiritual awakening as a result of these steps, we try to carry this message to other addicts and practice these principles in all our affairs.

<u>We pass it onl</u>

* * *

Chapter 19

Preventing Relapse

1. Remember God is with you. Don't resurrect the old life!

He will give you the strength you need to resist your temptations, and the tools to overcome them.

2. To avoid relapse, you need to choose to quit and stay quit, otherwise you've never really started recovery.

But if you choose to quit and stay quit, be careful not to resurrect the old life. For example, if you're addicted to alcohol, don't go sit in a bar! People in recovery sometimes set themselves up by putting themselves back in harm's way. Say someone accepts and admits their use of crack cocaine caused the majority of unmanageability in their lives, but they leave the door open to the possibility of having a few beers once in a while because, in their addictive thinking, drinking didn't cause as much damage. Likewise, some recovering alcoholics will sometimes substitute marijuana or other mood-altering chemicals (prescribed medication) to help them deal with life on its own terms. The NA literature says it well when it states:

3. "This is a program of abstinence from all drugs."

Abstinence and the desire to do what is necessary to abstain from all addictive substances and behaviour, is recovery. Substitution is not! It only leads to more delusion and consequences. You'll reap what you sow don't get cocky. Remember: God favours the humble. "Be careful! Watch out for attacks from the Devil, your great enemy. He prowls around like a roaring lion, looking for some victim to devour" (1 Peter 5:8, NLT). He would like nothing better than to help you destroy your testimony, your life and the lives of your family.

4. I hope by now you've found a church meeting place (a Christ-centred denomination).

If not, ask God to guide you so you can participate with other followers of Jesus in furthering His Kingdom

5. Apart from prayer and meditation, worshipping with other believers is very important in your walk with God.

You need to connect with other believers so you can further God's Kingdom through your spiritual gifts, talents and finances. Get involved with your church community.

6. Don't start a relationship with the opposite sex too early in recovery!

This is a major cause of relapse. Why? Because in early recovery, you lack emotional management skills. So when the normal problems in a relationship happen, you dramatize it, become resentful, and get into self-pity, which is a great place to revert to your old skills – escaping through mood-altering behaviour.

7. If and when you do get into a serious relationship with the opposite sex, find a godly couple.

Ask if you can get advice from them from time to time to help you and your partner succeed with your relationship.

8. Dealing with resentment.

The practice of unforgiveness fuels the lust for vindication. These create overwhelming feelings which lead to relapse. When resentment comes, acknowledge the hurt you're experiencing through real or perceived behaviour of others. Then, confess your anger and lust for vindication to God, and ask Him to forgive you and take it away. If you need to apologize to someone for your part, do it quickly and move on. When those feelings come back after you've dealt with them, refuse to give them power. Set your mind on things above.

There will be times when you experience unfair treatment, often from friends and even other Christians. In life, at times you'll go through dark valleys and wonder if living is worth the trouble.

Others times, you'll experience betrayal, rejection, persecution, etc. Renew your mind. "The righteous face many troubles, but the LORD rescues them from each and every one" (Psalm 34:19, NLT).

In those difficult times, push through! Worship God! You're not controlled by mood altering behaviours anymore – you have choices! So put some music on, go to a worship service, read Psalm 13, and do what it says. Some of us have learned when we're having problems, we're too focused on ourselves. So go and do something for somebody else. Get out of yourself! And do it for the love of God and the love of others.

9. Choose to forgive.

Yes! Forgiveness is a choice. You may have to do it repeatedly for a period of time, but follow Jesus' commandment. Pray for your enemies and those who curse you. You'll be rewarded if you follow His way of doing things.

10. Practice humility!

Pride is something that needs to be put to death. Some people in recovery are more concerned about saving face than saving their behinds. "Do nothing out of selfish ambition or vain conceit, but in humility consider others better (*more important*) than yourselves" (Philippians 2:3, NIV). Why? Because that is what Jesus did!

11. Leadership training.

If you're a leader, remember Christian leadership is about obeying God and at times washing the feet of the people you lead.

12. Practice gratitude.

In spite of everything, choose to believe God loves you, He is in you and with you always. So give Him thanks!

What is "**preventing relapse**"? It's the practice of unselfishness. It's shouldering our problems and responsibilities without the use of mood-altering chemicals or behaviours. It's also loving God and others by following the path Jesus has set before us.

It's growing to realize He is with you, that he cares about you, and that without Him, you can do nothing of any godly value.

Renew your mind. Study Jesus' words. Apply them to your life. Continue to depend on His Holy Spirit to help you live the Christian life. When you do this, you'll experience His abundant life.

Finally, trust in the Lord and do good by doing His will.

Chapter 20

A New Beginning

"I pray that the God who gives hope will fill you with much joy and peace while you trust in him. Then your hope will overflow by the power of the Holy Spirit" (Romans 15:13, NCV).

Take a minute, and remember what situations brought you to the point of admitting you were powerless over your addiction and that your life had become unmanageable.

Now think about how far you've come from those experiences. What I want to convey to you, to encourage you with, is this is only the beginning. As you continue to focus on the mercy and grace (Power) of God and let go of the past, you can expect to grow spiritually, mentally, emotionally, social and physically.

I want to be careful here. I don't want to give you the impression that by following Jesus, you'll have no problems. You will, as a matter of fact. You'll have great challenges at times. But remember God is with you always, in times of joy and times of trouble.

Spiritually, your desire to find out more about God the Father and His Son, Jesus Christ, will increase. As you continue to read, study and apply God's Word to your life, you'll develop wisdom (a Christian mind) that empowers you for intimacy with the Creator of heaven and earth. God's Spirit will communicate with you in ways that non-believers will envy. Your understanding of forgiveness, mercy, peace and grace for yourself and others will come to life. You know that "high" – the feeling you were looking for through mind-altering behaviours? You'll surpass it, but it'll be through your intimacy with the Lord Jesus Christ who lives in you.

"The Lord is my helper" will become a reality through many situations you'll experience. I know this sounds far-fetched, but you'll get to appreciate His discipline and understand the Lord disciplines those He loves.

Spending time with God through worship, prayer and meditation will become a necessity, just like spending time with a loving spouse. Wanting His advice and direction will become a pursuit. Seeking His encouragement through godly people, places and things will become the normality of your Christian walk. God's power will heal so many areas of your life, you'll become a different person. A new creation.

Mentally, you'll think better. So much so, you'll realize how stupid and unimportant some of your past thinking was before God began to renew your mind. You'll develop a "Christian mind." Your discernment of right and wrong will mature. Your self-centred thinking will decrease. You'll think godly thoughts like, "People matter to God, so they need to matter to me." "At times, I need to consider others as more important than myself, so I need to love them." "As much as it depends on me, I need to be at peace with everyone." "I'll forgive others because Jesus forgives all my sins. I'll pray for my enemies." By allowing God to change the way you think, you'll have the opportunity to make better choices.

Emotionally, your feelings of love for God and others will intensify. You'll become more positive and experience less self-pity. At times, you'll experience a sense of hope and joy through the power of God's Spirit. You'll become more patient (long-suffering) and experience more peace. You'll become kinder, more faithful to God and others. You'll develop integrity and be more trusting of God and others. Through the Spirit of God, you'll experience self-control and become more tolerant of yourself and others. You'll become gentler and have a strong desire to do what is good (God's will).

Socially, you'll develop healthier relationships. Others will seek you out, and not because you owe them money, but because they want to be with you. If you're single and it's God's will for you to marry, you'll find a lifetime partner, and will apply yourself to loving this person (of the opposite sex) for the rest of your life. If you're presently married and choosing because of God's Word to stay married, trusting in His mercy and grace, you'll rebuild your marriage relationship. Your parents, grandparents, spouse, children and grandchildren will become more trusting of you. Because of the changes God is doing in your life, they'll be grateful and experience more peace. The bottom line? You'll become less self-centred and so much more enjoyable to be around.

Physically, this is usually the part that gets better faster than the other areas of your life. Of course, because of the seriousness of your addiction, you may be experiencing a multitude of ailments. But because you don't live that old lifestyle anymore, quite a few of those ailments will get better. As you quit one addiction, you may become aware that other compulsive behaviours will rear their ugly heads. Be patient with yourself. You'll develop better eating habits and hopefully sleeping habits too. But it'll take time. Something you won't experience anymore if drinking or drugging was your addiction, are the come downs and hangovers.

Finally, in this world you *will* have problems. But because of God's power and your determination, you'll be able to deal with them without reverting to your mood-altering behaviours. So trust in the Lord, do good, don't resurrect those old behaviours, and you'll experience the abundant life that Jesus promises.

"With God's power working in us, God can do much, much more than anything we can ask or imagine. To him be glory in the church and in Christ Jesus for all time, forever and ever. Amen" (Ephesians 3:20-21, NCV).

Ingram Content Group UK Ltd.
Milton Keynes UK
UKHW010616060623
422946UK00001B/38

9 781613 793800